I did it "His Way"

Personal Testimony written by
Elizabeth Das

"THIS BOOK is rated "A" in christian and religious world"

Republished in 2018 and 2023

Contact:nimmidas@gmail.com
nimmidas1952@gmail.com

YouTube Channel "Daily Spiritual Diet Elizabeth Das

https://waytoheavenministry.org

1. youtube.com/@dailyspiritualdietelizabet7777/videos

2. youtube.com/@newtestamentkjv9666/videos

This book is available in five languages in Paperback, Ebook and audio.

FOREWARD

"For my thoughts are not your thoughts, neither are your ways my ways, said the LORD. For as the heavens are higher than the earth, so are my ways higher than your ways, and my thoughts than your thoughts." (Isaiah 55:8-9)

This book is a composition of memories and short testimonies by Ms. Elizabeth Das who has dedicated herself to the ministry of evangelizing and teaching the Word of the Lord. Seeking "His way" through determination and the Power of prayer, Ms. Das will take you on a personal journey through her own life changing experiences. Born and raised in India, Ms. Das worshiped regularly at the family alter. She was not satisfied with religion as her heart told her that there had to be more to God. She frequently visited churches and joined religious organizations but was never fully satisfied.

One day she set out to find truth in a distant country far from her native home, India. Her journey begins in Ahmadabad, India where she had a profound desire to find the One True God. Due to the liberties in America at the time and away from the religious cultures and traditions of her homeland, Ms. Das traveled to America with the purpose of finding the truth of this Living God. Not that you cannot find God anywhere but America, because God is all present and omnipotent. This, however, was where the Lord took Ms. Das as this book will explain the road to her salvation and of her profound love for the lover of her soul.

"Ask and it shall be given you; seek, and ye shall find; knock, and it shall be opened unto you. For every one that asketh receiveth; and he that seeketh findeth; and to him that knocketh it shall be opened." (Matthew 7:7-8)

I have personally known Ms. Das for close to 30 years when she first entered a small church that I attended in Southern California. The love for her homeland and the people of India is an urgency-felt ministry for

Ms. Das who has a deep desire for winning souls of all cultures and backgrounds to the Lord.

"The fruit of the righteous is a tree of life; and he that winneth souls is wise. (Proverbs 11:30)

Ms. Das actively works spreading the Word of God from her home based office in Wylie, Texas. You may visit her website at www.gujubible.org or waytoheavenministry.org where you can obtain Bible Studies translated from the English language to Gujarati. You can also find locations to churches in India. Pastors of these churches share the same love for the truth as Ms. Das. She networks with apostolic faith ministers within the United States and abroad for the purpose of acquiring guest speakers for the Annual Conferences that are held in India. Ms. Das' ministry and work in India are well known. They include the fruition of a pastoral Apostolic Bible College in India, an orphanage, and day care centers. From America, Ms. Das has assisted with the establishment of churches in India where many have come to know the Lord Jesus Christ. She is a woman of great faith, steady and unfailing in prayer. These accomplishments have been attained while totally dependent on God for everything and while living on disability. Her meager financial support is a testament of her strong will and determination that is greater than her means. Ms. Das will say with assurance, "God always provides and takes care of me." Yes, somehow He does and exceeds her needs abundantly!

Busy doing the Lord's work from dawn to dusk, Ms. Das is always ready to pray with me or anyone who is in need of help. God is always the answer. She stands between that gap, instant in profound prayer, with authority and intercession. God does take care of Ms. Das because she has a love for evangelizing. She listens to His voice and will not go against "His Ways." Obedience is greater than sacrifice, obedience with a passion to please God.

This is the appointed time for writing this book. God is the "Great Strategist." His ways are perfect and meticulous. Things and situations do not happen before their appointed time. Pray for direction in hearing the mind and feeling the heart of God through the Holy Spirit. This book will continue to be written in the heart of the lives of men and women that she has influenced through His ways.

Rose Reyes,

The English name is I did it His Way.

The French name of the book is: Je l'ai fait à "sa manière"

The Spanish book name is 'Lo hice a "a Su manera"

Gujarati name is me te temni rite karyu.... મેં તે તેમની રીતે કર્યું

Hindi name is Maine uske tarike se kiya...मैंने उसके तरीके से किया

These books are also available in Audio and Ebook platforms.

Daily Spiritual Diet is a yearly Reading by Elizabeth Das Available in English, Gujarati, and Hindi. Ebook and paper book.

ACKNOWLEDGMENTS

I express my deepest appreciation: to my family and friends, especially my mom Esther Das. She is the greatest example of a Christian lady who has helped me further my ministry and always supports me in every direction it takes.

I give thanks to my friend Rose for supporting me and helping to put parts of this book together.

I also would like to thank my prayer partner Sister Veneda Ing, for making herself available to me any and all the time; but mostly I thank her for her fervent prayers.

I thank God for all who have been such a great help in translating and editing. I thank God for many others who gave their time to help me put this book together.

Table of Contents

THE WAYS OF THE LORD

• *As for God, his way is perfect: the word of the LORD is tried: he is a buckler to all those that trust in him. (Psalms 18:30)*

•   *But he knoweth the way that I take: when he hath tried me, I shall come forth as gold. My foot hath held his steps, his way have I kept, and not declined. Neither have I gone back from the commandment of his lips; I have esteemed the words of his mouth more than my necessary food. (Job 23:10-12)*

• *Wait on the LORD, and keep his way, and he shall exalt thee to inherit the land: when the wicked are cut off, thou shalt see it. (Psalms 37:34)*

• *The LORD is righteous in all his ways, and holy in all his works. (Psalms 145:17)*

• *The LORD shall establish thee a holy people unto himself, as he hath sworn unto thee, if thou shalt keep the commandments of the LORD thy God, and walk in his ways. (Deuteronomy 28:9)*

• *And many people shall go and say, come ye, and let us go up to the mountain of the LORD, to the house of the God of Jacob; and he will teach us of his ways, and we will walk in his paths: for out of Zion shall go forth the law, and the word of the LORD from Jerusalem. (Isaiah 2:3)*

• *The meek will he guide in judgment: and the meek will he teach his way. (Psalms 25:9)*

Book Referencing: HOLY BIBLE, King James Version

Chapter 1

The Beginning: In Search For The Spirit Of Truth.

I n June of 1980, I came to the United States of America with a strong desire to find the truth about God the creator of all things. It was not as though I could not find God in India because God is everywhere and fills the universe with His presence and glory; but this was not enough for me. I wanted to know Him personally, if it were possible.

"And I heard as it were the voice of a great multitude, and as the voice of many waters, and as the voice of mighty thunderings, saying, Alleluia: for the Lord God omnipotent reigneth." (Revelation 19:6)

I was on an extraordinary journey when God led me to the United States of America. I thought it was where I had chosen to go, but time proved me wrong. I came to understand that God had more to do with this decision than I realized. It was "His Way" of changing my thoughts and life.

America is a country that offers freedom of religion, a fusion of multicultural people, with liberties and protection to those who desire to exercise religious rights without the fear of persecution. I began taking leaps over unsettled waters in this country as God began to direct me. It was as though He was laying stepping- stones to guide me. These "stones" were what set the foundation for a long and tumultuous journey leading to revelation where there would be no turning back. The reward would be worth living by His Ways, at every turn and test of my faith.

"I press toward the mark for the prize of the high calling of God in Christ Jesus. Let us therefore, as many as be perfect, be thus minded: and if in anything ye be otherwise minded, God shall reveal even this unto you. Nevertheless, whereto we have already attained, let us walk by the same rule, let us mind the same thing." (Philippians 3:14-16)

When I arrived in California, I did not see many Eastern Indians during this time. I adjusted to life in America and focused on what I was here for. I was searching for the Living God of the Bible, the God of the apostles John, Peter and Paul and others who carried the cross and followed Jesus.

I ventured to find the God of the New Testament who did many marvelous miracles, signs and wonders according to the Holy Bible, the Word of the Living God. Could I be so presumptuous to even think that he really knew me? There had to be more to God. I began visiting many churches of various denominations within the Los Angeles area, a metropolis located in Southern California. I later moved to a city east of Los Angeles called West Covina and began visiting churches in that area as well. I came from a very religious country with probably more gods known to man than any other country in the world. I always believed in one God, the Creator. My heart sought to know him in a personal way. I thought, surely He does exist and He will be able to find me because of my passionate desire to know him personally. I sought relentlessly and read the Bible consistently but something was always missing. I obtained employment at the United States Postal Office in August 1981 where I began asking my co-workers questions about God. I also began listening to Christian radio where I heard different preachers discussing biblical topics and yet never agreeing even among themselves. I thought, surely this could not be a God of confusion? There had to be a truthful answer to this religious quandary. I knew I had to search the Holy Scriptures and continue to pray. Many Christian coworkers also spoke to me and shared their testimony. I was surprised that they knew so much about The Lord. I did not know then that God had already set a time for me to receive the revelation of His marvelous truth.

My brother was afflicted with demonic possession and needed a miracle. I was compelled to look for Bible-believing Christians who believed in miracles and deliverance from these demonic forces. Without mercy, these demonic spirits were tormenting my brother's mind. My family was extremely concerned for him that we had no alternative but to take him to a psychiatrist. I knew it was the devil's pleasure to torment and destroy my brother. This was the spiritual warfare as spoken in the Bible. In desperation we took my brother to the psychiatrist. After having assessed him, she asked us if we believed in Jesus. We said yes that we did then she began to write down addresses to two churches with their telephone numbers and handed them to me. Once at home, I placed both papers with the information on my dresser with the intention of calling both pastors. I prayed that God would lead me to the right church and pastor. I heard of some very negative things concerning churches in America, so this made me very cautious. The Lord uses prophets, teachers and preachers to lead those who love him to all truth. The Lord became my Lamp and Light that brightened my darkness. God would surely lead my brother out of his darkness too. I truly believed that God would find me in what seemed like an endless sea of darkness; because this was a very dark and difficult time for my family.

"Thy word is a lamp unto my feet, and a light unto my path."
(Psalms 119:105)

"Prayer and Fasting."

I placed both the addresses on my dresser. I called both pastors and had a communication with both of them. Simultaneously, I was praying for the direction from the Lord for the pastor to which I could continue my conversation. During this time, I realized that one number from the dresser disappeared. I carefully searched for it but could not find it. Now only one number was available for me. I called that number and spoke to the pastor of the church located in, California just 10 minutes from my home. I took my brother to this church thinking my brother will be free today but it did not happen that way. My brother was not completely delivered that day. So the pastor offered us a Bible study. We took him up on his offer and also began attending his church with no intention of becoming a member, but only a visitor. Little did I know that this would be the turning point of my life. At this time, I was against the Pentecostal way and their belief of speaking in tongues.

The saints of the church were very sincere in their beliefs. They worshipped freely and obeyed the pastor when he called for a fast because the spiritual forces that controlled my brother would only come out, as the Word of God says, "by prayer and fasting". Once, the disciples of Jesus could not cast out a demon. Jesus told them it was because of their unbelief and said that nothing shall be impossible to them.

"Howbeit this kind goeth not out but by prayer and fasting."
(Matthew 17:21)

We all fasted a few days at a time on several occasions, and I could see that my brother was getting much better. We continued having Bible studies in my home with the pastor, understanding everything that he taught us; however, when he began to explain water Baptism, I was bothered by his interpretation. I had never heard of the baptism in the name of "Jesus", although he clearly showed us the scriptures. It was written there but I did not see it. Maybe, my understanding had been blinded.

After the pastor left, I turned to my brother saying, "Did you notice that all preachers using the same Bible come up with different ideas? I really don't believe what these preachers are saying anymore." My brother turned to me saying, "He is right!" I became very upset with my brother and asked him, "So you're going to believe this pastor's teaching? I do not believe this." He looked at me again and said, "He is telling the truth." I responded again, "You believe all preachers but not me!" Again my brother insisted, "He is right." This time I could see that my brother's face was very serious. I later took the Bible and began studying the Book of Acts where the history of the early church was. I studied and studied; I still could not see why, God had HIS WAY. Do you believe that God deals with each person differently? Here I was searching for God through every source and media. During this time, I heard God speaking to my heart, "You need to be baptized." I heard His command and hid these words in my heart unknown to anyone else.

The day came when the Pastor walked up to me and asked me a question, "So now, are you ready to be baptized?" I looked at the him with surprise never having anyone ask me this question before. He told me that the Lord Jesus had spoken to him about my baptism, so I said, "yes". I was amazed that God would speak to the Pastor about this matter. I left the church thinking, "I hope God isn't telling this him everything since our thoughts are not always righteous or even appropriate."

Baptism for the Remission of Sin.

The day of my baptism arrived. I asked the pastor to make sure he baptized me in the name of the Father, of the Son and of the Holy Ghost. The pastor kept telling me, "Yes that is the name of Jesus." I was worried and upset; I thought this man will send me to hell if he does not baptize me in the name of Father, Son and Holy Ghost. So I repeated myself to him again to please make sure that he invoked in the name of the Father, and of the Son and of the Holy Ghost, but the pastor kept repeating himself as well. "Yes, his name is Jesus." I began to think that this Pastor really didn't understand what I meant. Since God had spoken to me about getting baptized, I could not disobey Him. I did not understand this at the time, but I was obeying God without having the full revelation of His name, nor did I fully understand that Salvation is by no other name but in the Name of Jesus.

"Neither is there salvation in any other; for there is none other name under heaven given among men whereby we must be saved."
(Acts 4:12)

"Ye are my witnesses saith the Lord and my **servant** *whom I have chosen: that ye may know and believe me and understand that I am he: before me there was no God formed neither shall there be after me. I, even I, am the Lord; and beside me there is* **no saviour.***"*
(Isaiah 43:10-11)

Before, after and forever, there was, is and will be only but one God and Saviour. Here a man will be as the role of servant, Jehovah God says that **I am he**.

Who, being in the form of God, thought it not robbery to be equal with God: But made himself of no reputation, and took upon him the form of a servant, and was made in the likeness of men: And being found in fashion as a man, he humbled himself, and became obedient unto death, even the death of the cross. (Philippians 2:6-8)

Jesus was the God, in human body.

And without controversy great is the mystery of godliness:
God was manifest in the flesh, *(1 Timothy 3:16)*

Why did this one God, who was spirit, come in the flesh? As you know, spirit does not have flesh and blood. If He needed to shed blood, then He would need a human body.

The Bible says:

*Take heed therefore unto yourselves, and to all the flock, over the which the Holy Ghost hath made you overseers, to feed the **church of God**, which he hath purchased with **his own blood**. (Acts 20:28)*

Most churches do not teach the oneness of God and the power of the name of Jesus. God, a Spirit in the flesh as the man Christ Jesus, gave the great commission to His disciples:

*"Go ye therefore and teach all nations baptizing them in the **name** (singular) of the Father and of the Son and of the Holy Ghost."*
(Matthew 28:19)

The disciples clearly knew what Jesus meant, because they went out baptizing in His Name, as it is written in the scriptures. I was amazed that they pronounced "In the Name of **Jesus**" each time they performed a baptism. Scriptures support this in the Book of Acts.

That day I was baptized in water in full submersion in the name of Jesus, I came out of the water feeling so light as though I could walk on water. A heavy mountain of sin had been removed. I did not know that I was carrying this heaviness on me. What a marvelous experience! I realized for the first time in my life, that I had been calling myself a "Christian with small sins," because I never felt that I was a big sinner. Regardless of what I believed, sin was still sin. I was doing and thinking sin. I no longer believed solely in God's existence but experienced joy and true Christianity by partaking in what the Word of God said.

I went back to the Bible again and started searching the same scripture. Guess what? He opened my understanding and I saw clearly for the first time, that Baptism is only in the NAME OF JESUS.

Then opened he their understanding, that they might understand the scriptures (Luke 24:45)

I started seeing scripture so clearly and thought how conniving Satan is to just wipe out the plan of The Most High God, who came in flesh to shed blood. The blood is hidden under the Name of **JESUS**. I found out right away that Satan's attack was on The Name.

*"Repent and be baptized each and every one of you in the **name of Jesus Christ** for the remission (FORGIVENESS) of sins and ye shall receive the gift of the Holy Ghost." (Acts 2:38)*

These words were what the Apostle Peter spoke on the Day of Pentecost at the beginning of the early church in the New Testament. After my baptism I received the gift of the Holy Ghost in one of my friend's church in Los Angeles.

This was manifested by my speaking in an unknown language or tongues and according to the Scriptures on the subject of the baptism of the Holy Ghost:

*"While Peter yet spake these words, the Holy Ghost fell on all them which heard the word. And they of the circumcision which believed were astonished as many as came with Peter because that on the Gentiles also was poured out the gift of the Holy Ghost. For they heard them **speak with tongues** and magnify God." (Acts 10: 44-46)*

I understood clearly that men had changed the baptismal ceremony. This is why we have so many religions today. These early believers were baptized according to the Scriptures that were later written. Peter preached it and the apostles performed it!

*"Can any man forbid water that these should not be baptized which have received the Holy Ghost as well as we? And he commanded them to be **baptized in the name of the Lord**. Then prayed they him to tarry certain days." (Acts 10:47-48)*

Again, evidence of Baptism in Jesus' Name.

*But when they believed Philip preaching the things concerning the kingdom of God, **and the name of Jesus Christ, they were baptized, both men and women**(For as yet he was fallen upon none of them: **only they were baptized in the name of the Lord Jesus**).(Acts8:12,16)*

Acts 19

*And it came to pass, that, while Apollos was at Corinth, Paul having passed through the upper coasts came to Ephesus: and finding certain disciples, He said unto them, Have ye received the Holy Ghost since ye believed? And they said unto him, We have not so much as heard whether there be any Holy Ghost. And he said unto them, Unto what then were ye baptized? And they said, Unto John's baptism. Then said Paul, John verily baptized with the baptism of repentance, saying unto the people, that they should believe on him which should come after him, that is, on Christ Jesus. When they heard this, they were **baptized in the name of the Lord Jesus**. And when Paul had laid his hands upon them, **the Holy Ghost came on them; and they spake with tongues**, and prophesied. (Acts 19:1-6)*

*Acts 19 was a big help to me, because the Bible says there is **One baptism**. (Ephesians 4:5)*

I was baptized in India and, I must say here, that I was sprinkled and not baptized.

The true doctrine was established by the **apostles and the prophets**. Jesus came to shed the blood and set an example. (1Peter 2:21)

*Acts 2:42 And they continued stedfastly in the **apostles' doctrine** and fellowship, and in breaking of bread, and in*
*Ephesians-2:20 And are **built upon the foundation of the apostles and prophets**, Jesus Christ himself being the chief corner stone;*

Galatians. 1:8, 9 But though we, or an angel from heaven, preach any other gospel unto you than that which we have preached unto you, let him be accursed. As we said before, so say I now again, if any man preach any other gospel unto you than that ye have received, let him be accursed.

(This is profound; no one can change the doctrine not even the Apostles who were already established.)

These scriptures opened my eyes, now I understood Mathew 28:19. Church is The Bride of Jesus,when we are baptized in the name of Jesus we then take on His Name. Song of Solomon is an allegory of the church and groom, in which the bride has taken on the Name.

*Because of the savour of thy good ointments **thy name is as ointment poured forth**, therefore do the virgins love thee (Song of Soloman 1:3)*

Now I had the baptism as spoken of in the Bible and the same Holy Ghost. This was not something that was imaginary; it was real! I could feel it and hear it and others witnessed the manifestation of the new-birth. The words that I uttered, I did not know nor could I understand. It was awesome.

*"For he that speaketh in an **unknown tongue** speaketh not unto men but unto God: for no man understandeth him howbeit in the spirit he speaketh mysteries." (I Corinthians 14:2)*

*"For if I pray in an unknown tongue, my spirit prayeth, but my **understanding is unfruitful.**" (I Corinthians 14:14)*

My mom testified that a time before I was born, a missionary from South India baptized her in a river and coming up, she was completely healed. Not knowing how this preacher baptized her, I wondered how she was healed. Years later my father confirmed to me, that this pastor baptized her in Jesus' Name, which is Biblical.

The Bible says:

"Who forgiveth all thine iniquities; who healeth all thy diseases;"

(Psalms 103:3)

After my new birth, I began giving Bible Studies to friends at work and to my family. My nephew received the gift of the Holy Ghost. My brother, cousin, and aunt were baptized along with many of my family members. Little did I know, there was much more to this journey, than only a desire to know God more intimately. I did not realize that this experience was possible. God dwells inside the believer through the Spirit.

Revelation and Understanding.

I Dedicated to studying the Holy Scriptures and reading the Bible repeatedly, God kept opening my understanding.

> *"Then opened He their understanding that they might understand the Scriptures." (Luke 24:45)*

After receiving the Holy Ghost my understanding became clearer as I began to learn and see many things that I had not seen before.

> *"But God hath **revealed** them unto **us by his Spirit**: for the Spirit searcheth all things, yea, the deep things of God." (1 Corinthians 2:10)*

I learned that we must have the understanding of His will for us, the wisdom to live by His Word, to know of **"His Ways"**, and to accept that obedience is a requirement and not an option.

One day I asked God, "How are you using me?" He told me "In prayer"

Wherefore the rather, brethren, give diligence to make your calling and election sure: for if ye do these things, ye shall never fall:
(2 Peter 1:10)

I learned that going to church could give one a sense of False security. Religion is not salvation. Religion of itself can only make you feel good about your own self righteousness. Knowing Scripture alone does not bring Salvation. You must understand the Holy Scriptures through study, receive revelation through prayer, and have a desire to know the truth. The devil knows scripture too and he is doomed to an eternity in the lake that burns with fire. Do not be deceived by wolves in sheep's clothing that have a **form of godliness** but **deny** the ***power of God***. No one ever told me I needed the Holy Ghost with the evidence of speaking in tongues, as spoken of in the Bible. When believers receive the Holy Spirit, something miraculous happens. The disciples were filled with the Holy Ghost and with fire.

*But ye shall receive **power**, after that the Holy Ghost is come upon you: and ye shall be witnesses unto me both in Jerusalem, and in all Judaea, and in Samaria, and unto the uttermost part of the earth. (Acts1:8)*

They were so much on fire to spread the gospel, that many Christians of that time, as some do even today, lost their lives for the Gospel of truth. I learned that this is a profound faith and a solid doctrine, unlike doctrine that is taught in some churches today.

After resurrection Jesus says in His word, this will be the sign of one being HIS DISCIPLE.

"....they shall speak with new tongues;" (Mark 16:17)

Tongue in the Greek language is glossa, in English, Supernatural gift of language given by God. You do not go to school to learn this way of speaking. That is why it says a **New Tongue.**

This is one of the signs to recognize the disciple of the Most High God.

Isn't God so wonderful? He made His disciples to be recognized in a very special way.

Power of Worship.

I learned about the power of worshipping and that you can actually feel a Holy presence in worship. When I came to America in 1980, I observed East Indians ashamed to freely worship God. In the Old Testament, King David danced, jumped, clapped and raised His hands high before the Lord. The Glory of God comes when the people of God worship with the highest of praise and exaltation. The people of God create the atmosphere for the Lord's presence to dwell among them. Our worship sends a savoring scent to the Lord that He cannot resist. He will come and dwell in the praises of His people. After prayer, take time to just praise and worship him with all of your heart without asking Him for things or favors. In the Bible, He is compared to a Groom coming for His bride (the church). He is looking for a passionate bride that will not be ashamed to WORSHIP HIM. I learned that we could offer worship that will reach the Throne Room if we let go of our pride. Thank God for preachers that preach the Word and do not hold back on how very important worship is to God.

"But the hour cometh, and now is, when the true Worshippers shall Worship the Father in spirit and in truth: for the Father seeketh such to Worship him." (John 4:23)

When God's presence descends upon His children, miracles begin to happen: healing, deliverance, tongues and interpretations, prophesy, manifestations of the gifts of the spirit. Oh how much power of God can we contain in one church service if we can all come together offering worship and exaltation and the highest of praise. When you no longer have words to pray, worship and offer the sacrifice of praise! The devil hates it when you worship his Creator, the One True God. When you feel alone or fear tugs at you, worship and connect yourself to God!

In the beginning this type of worship and praise was very hard for me, but later it became easy. I began hearing His voice speaking to me. He wanted me to be obedient to His Spirit. My religious background had kept me from worshiping God freely. Soon I was getting blessed in the

Spirit, healing came, and I was delivered from things that I had not seen as sin. This was all new to me; each time I felt the presence of God in my life I began to change inwardly. I was growing and experiencing a Christ-centered personal walk with God.

Spirit of Truth.

Love for truth is essential because religion can be deceptive and worse than an addiction to alcohol or drugs.

> *"God is a Spirit: and they that worship him must Worship him in spirit and in truth." (John 4:24)*

The chains of bondage to religion fell off me when the Holy Ghost set me free. When we speak in unknown tongues or languages in the Holy Ghost, our spirit speaks to God. God's love is overwhelming and the experience is supernatural. I could not help to think about all those years before, when I received Bible doctrine that was contrary to the Word of God.

In my relationship with God, He revealed more truth as I grew in His Word and learned of "**His Ways.**" It was like the sparrow that feeds her young with small portions, they grow stronger and consistently each day, until they have learned to soar the skies. Seek the Spirit of Truth and He will guide you to know all things. One day, we too will soar the heavens with the Lord.

> *"When The Spirit of truth is come, He will guide you into all truth." (John 16:13a)*

Holy Unction:

Through much sorrow because of my brother's condition with evil spirits, we found this marvelous truth. I embraced this truth and the Holy Spirit gave me power to overcome obstacles that interfered with my new life in Christ Jesus that gave me the holy unction to operate and minister by teaching people. I learnt that through this unction, God moved through spiritual fervour and expression. It comes from the Holy One, being God Himself and not a religious rite or formal ordination giving one this privilege.

The Anointing:

I began to feel the anointing of God on my life and witnessed to those who would listen. I found myself becoming a teacher of the Word through God's anointing power. There was a time in India when I wanted to practice law but the Lord turned me into a teacher of His Word.

"But the anointing which ye have received of him abideth in you, and ye need not that any man teaches you: but as the same anointing teacheth you of all things, and is truth, and is no lie, and even as it hath taught you, ye shall aide in him." (1 John 2:27)

"But ye have an unction from the Holy One, and ye know all things." (1 John 2:20)

I made myself available to God and He did the rest through His anointing power. What an awesome God! He will not leave you powerless in doing His work. I began to pray more as my body became weak due to illness and disease but the Spirit of God in me grew stronger each day as I put time and effort into my Spiritual walk praying, fasting and reading His Word constantly.

Life Change:

Looking back for a moment, I saw where God had brought me from and how my life had been void of His ways. I had a carnal nature with no power to change it. I had other spirits but not the Holy Spirit. I learned that prayer changes things but the true miracle was that I had also changed. I wanted my ways to be more like **His ways** so I fasted to change my carnal nature. My life had changed significantly on this road traveled, but it had just begun as my passionate desire for God increased. Others who knew me well, could testify that I had changed.

Spiritual Warfare:

I was careful to teach only truth and not religion. I taught the baptism in the Name of Jesus Christ and the Holy Spirit of God (Holy Ghost) is a necessity. It is the Comforter and your power to overcome obstacles and the evil forces that come against believers.

Be ready always, to fight on your knees for what you want from God. The devil wants to crush you and your family. We are at war with the powers of darkness. We must fight for the souls to be saved; and pray that the heart of the sinner be touched by God so they may turn away from the powers that rule over them.

"For we wrestle not against flesh and blood, but against principalities, against powers, against the rulers of the darkness of this world, against spiritual wickedness in high places."
(Ephesians 6:12)

A Living Soul.

Everyone has a living soul; it is not your own, it belongs to God. One day when we die, the soul will return to God or Satan. Man can kill the body but only God can kill the soul.

*"Behold, all souls are mine; as the soul of the father, so also the soul of the son is mine: the soul that sinneth, it shall **die**."*
(Ezekiel 18:4)

"And fear not them which kill the body, but are not able to kill the soul: but rather fear him which is able to destroy both soul and body in hell." (Matthew 10:28)

Spirit of Love.

One life means so much to God because He cares and loves each one of us so much. Believers who have this Gospel of Truth are held accountable for telling others about the love of Jesus in the Spirit of **Love**.

> *"A new commandment I give unto you, That ye **love** one another; as I have **loved** you, that ye also **love** one another. By this shall all men know that ye are my disciples, if ye have **love** one to another."*
> *(John 13:34-35)*

The devil will come against us when we become a threat to him. It is his job to discourage us; however, we have the promise of victory over him.

> *"But thanks be to God, which giveth us the victory through our Lord Jesus Christ." (1 Corinthians 15:57)*

Let me stress here that, what Satan meant to be evil, God turned into the blessing.

The Bible says:

> *"And we know that all things work together for good to them that love God, to them who are the called according to his purpose."*
> *(Roman 8:28)*

PRAISE be to The Lord Jesus Christ!

Chapter 2

The Mighty Physician

edical science reports that there are a total of thirty-nine categories of diseases. Take cancer for instance, there are so many types of cancer. There are also many types of fever but they all fall under the fever category. According to old Roman law and Moses law, you could not inflict more than 40 stripes, (lashings), as punishment. So as not to violate this Roman and Jewish law, they administered only thirty-nine stripes. Is it coincidence that Jesus took thirty-nine stripes on His back? I believe, as many do, that there is a correlation to this number and Jesus.

"Forty stripes he may give him, and not exceed: lest, if he should exceed, and beat him above these with many stripes, then thy brother should seem vile unto thee." (Deuteronomy 25:3)

"Who his own self bare our sins in his own body on the tree, that we, being dead to sin, should live unto righteousness: by whose stripes ye were healed." (1 Peter 2:24)

"But he was wounded for our transgressions, he was bruised for our iniquities: the chastisement of our peace was upon him; and with his stripes we are healed." (Isaiah 53:5)

Throughout this book, you will read testimonies regarding the healing power of God and the power of deliverance from drugs, alcohol and demonic possession. I begin with my own personal illnesses where God showed me early on, that nothing is too difficult or too big for him. He is the Mighty Physician. The severity of my physical condition changed from bad to worse through painful sicknesses. It was and is the Word of God and His promises that sustain me today.

Chronic Sinusitis.

I had a sinus problem that was so severe that it prevented me from sleeping. During the day I would call and ask people to pray for me. I would be fine for the moment but at night it would resume and I couldn't sleep.

One Sunday I went to church and asked the Pastor to pray for me. He laid his hand on my head and prayed over me.

"Is any sick among you? Let him call for the elders of the church; and let them pray over him, anointing him with oil in the name of the Lord:" (James 5:14)

When the worship service began, I started to praise and worship God as the spirit came on me so freely. The Lord told me to dance before him. In the Spirit I started dancing before Him in obedience when all of a sudden my stuffy nose loosened up and what was obstructing the nasal passages came out. Instantly I began to breath and this condition has not returned. I had accepted this sinus condition with my very own words and thoughts. However, eventually I learned that we should always speak out our faith and never confess or think doubt.

Tonsillitis.

I had chronic tonsillitis and could not sleep due to the horrible persistent pain. I suffered this condition for many years. After seeing a doctor; I was referred to a Hematologist. In order to perform what was a relatively minor tonsillectomy, it would be a dangerous and lengthy surgery for me because of a blood disease that made it difficult for my body to clot. In other words, I could bleed to death! The doctor said there wasn't any way that I could endure this operation or tolerate the pain. I prayed for my own healing and also asked the church to pray for me. One day a visiting preacher came to my church. He greeted the congregation and asked if anyone needed healing.

Uncertain about receiving my own healing, I made my way to the front anyway, trusting God. When I returned to my seat, I heard a voice telling me.

"You are not going to be healed."
I was angry at this voice. How could this voice boldly speak this doubt and unbelief? I knew this was a trick of the devil to stop my healing. I replied in opposition to this voice,

"I will get my healing!"

My response was firm and strong because I knew it came from the father of all lies, the devil. The Holy Ghost gives us authority over the devil and his angels. I was not about to allow him to rob me of my healing and peace. He is a liar and there is no truth in him! I was fighting back with the Word and promises of God.

> *"Ye are of your father the devil and the lusts of your father ye will do.*
> *He was a murderer from the beginning and abode not in the truth*
> *because there is no truth in him. When he speaketh a lie, he speaketh of*
> *is own: for he is a liar and the father of it." (John 8:44)*

Instantly my pain was gone and I was healed! Sometimes we have to go into the enemy's camp to fight for what we want and take back what the enemy, the devil, wants to take away from us. As the pain left me, the devil said, "You were not sick". The enemy was trying to convince me by a "cloud of doubt" that I had not really been sick. The reason for this lie of the devil was for me not to give God the Glory. With a firm answer to Satan, I said, "Yes I was sick!" Instantly Jesus put the pain on each side of my tonsils. I replied, "Lord Jesus, I know I was sick and you healed me." The pain left me forever! I never suffered again. Immediately I raised my hands, praised the Lord and gave God the glory. Jesus took stripes on his back so that I could be healed that day. His Word also says that my sins would also be forgiven. I stood up and testified to the church that very day how the Lord healed me. I took my healing by force.

"And from the days of John the Baptist until now the kingdom of heaven suffereth violence, and the violent take it by force."
(Matthew 11:12)

"And the prayer of faith shall save the sick and the Lord shall raise him up; and if he have committed sins, they shall be forgiven him."
(James 5:15)

"Who forgiveth all thine iniquities; who healeth all thy diseases."
(Psalms 103:3)

When we stand up and testify about what the Lord has done, we not only give God the Glory but it lifts the faith of others who need to hear it. Also it is fresh blood against the devil.

"And they overcame him by the blood of the Lamb, and by the word of their testimony; and they loved not their lives unto the death".
(Revelation 12:11)

God performs miracles both big and small. You defeat the devil when you tell others about what God has done for you. You make the devil run when you begin to worship God with all of your heart! You have weapons of faith and the power of the Holy Ghost available to defeat the father of all lies. We must learn to use them.

Vision Defect.

I had a problem with my vision in 1974, before I came to America. I could not differentiate distance between myself and another object in front of me. This caused severe headaches and nausea. The doctor said I had a retina condition that could be corrected with exercises; however, it did not work for me and my headaches continued.

I was attending a church in California that believed in healing power. I asked the church to pray for me. I kept hearing healing testimonies that helped me to believe for healing. I am so thankful that churches allowed testimonies, that others can hear praise reports of miracles that God has performed in the lives of ordinary people today. My faith was always lifted by hearing testimony. I learned a lot through Testimony.

I later went to see an eye doctor since God asked me to see the eye specialist.

This doctor examined my eyes and found the same problem but asked me to get a second opinion. A week later I asked for the prayer since I had a severe headache and unbearable pain in my eyes.

I went for second opinion, which examined my eyes, said that there was nothing wrong with my eyes. I was very happy.

Six month later, I was driving to work and thinking about what the doctor said and began trusting that nothing was wrong and the other doctor who diagnosed imperfection in the eyes was wrong. I was healed for all this months and forgot about how sick I was.

God began to speak to me,"Do you remember you had unbearable pain, a headache, and nausea?"

I said, "Yes." Then God said, "Do you remember when you were in India and the doctor said that you had an eye condition and you were taught eye coordination exercises? Do you recall that during the last six months you have not come home ill due to this problem?"

I responded, "Yes."

God said to me, "I healed your eyes!"

Praise God, this explained why the third doctor could not find anything wrong with me. God allowed me to go through this experience to show me that He is able to go deep into my eyes and heal them. The Word of God says, "I know the heart, not the one who owns the heart." I carefully began to ponder on these words in my mind. I may own my heart, but I do not know my own heart nor do I know what I have in my heart. For this reason I pray, fast and read the Word continually so that God may only find goodness, love and faith in my heart. We must be careful with what we think and what comes out of our mouth. Meditate on goodness because God knows our very thought.

> *"Let the words of my mouth, and the meditation of my heart, be acceptable in thy sight, O LORD, my strength, and my redeemer." (Psalms 19:14)*

> *"The heart is deceitful above all things and desperately wicked: who can know it? I the Lord search the heart, I try the reins, even to give every man according to his ways and according to the fruit of his doings."(Jeremiah 17:9-10)*

I pray Psalms 51 for me:

> *"Create in me a clean heart, O God; and renew a right spirit within me.(Psalms 51:10)*

Anxiety.

I was going through a period where I experienced something that I could not put into words. I remember telling God that I did not know why I was feeling this way in my mind. I prayed and asked God that I could not understand this overwhelming feeling because I was not worried about anything at that time. This feeling lasted for some time and it made me feel "off" mentally but not physically which is the best way I can describe it. Later at work, I had this small inspiration book in my hand.

The Lord said, "Open this book and read."

I found the topic on "anxiety." God said that what you have is anxiety. I was not familiar with this word. Since I did not have a clear understanding of this word, Jesus said look in the dictionary. I found the exact symptoms I was having. The definition was concern or solicitude respecting some thing or event, future or uncertain, which disturbs the mind, and keeps it in a state of painful uneasiness.

I said, "Yes Lord, I feel exactly this way!"

I worked the swing shift and on my day off I would go to sleep early. During this time I used to wake up early in the morning to pray and one day God told me to go to sleep. I thought, "Why would God say this?" At this early stage in my walk with God, I was learning to discern and hear His voice. Again I said to myself, why is God telling me to go to sleep? I think this is the devil.

Then I remembered that sometimes God says things to us that may not make any sense, but He is giving us an important message. In short, His message was that we do not need to be holier than thou.

"For my thoughts are not your thoughts, neither are your ways my ways, saith the LORD. For as the heavens are higher than the earth, so are my ways higher than your ways, and my thoughts than your thoughts". (Isaiah 55:8-9)

In other words, prayer is the right way but during that time, it was not. He already dispatched His Angel to minister to me and I needed to be in the bed. There is a time to rest and a time for God to refill our lamps with fresh oil through prayer renewing the Holy Ghost. In the natural, we need sleep and rest to refresh our bodies and mind as God intended. We are the Temple of God and need to take care of ourselves.

*But to which of **the angels** said he at any time, Sit on my right hand, until I make thine enemies thy footstool? Are they not all **ministering spirits, sent forth to minister for them who shall be heirs of salvation**? (Hebrews 1:13,14)*

When I went back to sleep again, I had a dream about a man without a head. The headless man touched my head. Later, I woke up feeling refreshed and totally normal; knowing God had sent a Healing Angel to touch my head and to deliver me from this anxiety. I was so thankful to God that I told everyone that would listen. I experienced the horrible debilitating symptoms of anxiety that had affected my mind. You wake up each day with it lingering; never giving you any peace because your mind is not fully rested to relax. Anxiety is also a tool of the devil to make you feel overwhelmed with fear or panic. It comes in many forms and you may not even know that you have it. The best thing to do is to change how you react to stress and ask yourself if you are giving your body what it needs to renew it daily. God will do the rest when you take care of "His Temple".

"If any man defile the temple of God, him shall God destroy; for the temple of God is holy, which temple ye are". (1 Corinthians 3:17)

His Voice.

When you have God, you are full because you are immersed in His love. The more you get to know Him, the more you love Him! The more you talk to him, the more you learn to hear his voice. The Holy Ghost helps you to discern the voice of God You just have to listen to that still small voice. We are the sheep of His pasture who know His voice.

"Then Jesus answered them, I told you, and ye believed not: the works that I do in my Father's name, they bear witness of me. But ye believe

not, because ye are not of my sheep, as I said unto you. My sheep hear my voice, and I know them, and they follow me: And I give unto them eternal life; and they shall never perish, neither shall any man pluck them out of my hand. My Father, which gave them me, is greater than all; and no man is able to pluck them out of my Father's hand. I and my Father are one." (John 10:25-30)

There are those of us who call ourselves His "sheep" and those who do not believe. His sheep hear God's voice. Religious demons are deceptive. They make us feel like we have God. The Holy Bible warns us about false doctrines.

> *"having a form of godliness but denying the power thereof."*
> *(2 Timothy3:5)*

God says, "seek me with all of your heart and you shall find me." It is not about finding a lifestyle that suits us. Follow truth, not religious tradition. If you are thirsty for God's truth, you will find it. You must read and love the Word of God, hide it in your heart and show it in your life-style. The Word changes you inwardly and outwardly.

Jesus came to break the power of tradition and the power of religion with the price of His Blood. He gave His life so that we could have forgiveness of sin and have direct communion with God. The Law was fulfilled in Jesus but they didn't confess Him as Lord and Savior, the Messiah.

> *"Nevertheless among the chief rulers also many believed on him; but because of the Pharisees they did not confess him, lest they should be put out of the synagogue: For they loved the praise of men more than the praise of God." (John 12:42, 43)*

Influenza:

I had a high fever accompanied by body aches. My eyes and face were also very swollen. I could barely speak and called the Elder of my church to pray for my healing. My facial features instantly became normal again and I was healed. I thank God for the men of faith and the assurance that He gives those who trust Him.

"For our gospel came not unto you in word only, but also in power and in the Holy Ghost and in much assurance." (1Thesalonians 1:5a)

Eye Allergy.

In Southern California we have a serious smog problem. I had an irritation in my eyes that became worse with the pollution in the air. The itching, redness, and constant pain was intolerable; it made me feel like taking my eyes out of their very socket. What a terrible way to feel. I was still growing and learning to trust God. I thought it was impossible for God to cure this even though He had already healed me in the past. I was just having a difficult time believing God for my healing. I was thinking that since God already knows my every thought He cannot heal my eyes because of my unbelief, so I used eye drops to ease the itching. The Lord began to speak to me to discontinue the eye drops. But the itching was very bad and I did not stop. He repeated this three times until I finally put the eye drops away.

*"But Jesus beheld them, and said unto them, With men this is impossible; but with **God all things are possible"**. (Matthew 19:26)*

A few hours later while I was at work, the itch left me. I was so happy that I began to tell everyone at work about my healing. I never had to worry about my eyes again. We know so little about God and how He thinks. We can never know Him because **His ways** are not our ways. Our knowledge of Him is so extremely small. This is why it is so crucial for true believers to walk in the Spirit. We cannot lean towards our own human understanding. Jesus was kind, patient, and merciful with me that day. Jesus was teaching me a great lesson. I had doubt for healing, but that day I obeyed and He healed me! He has never given up on me and He will never give up on you!

After this lesson on obedience, I put away all kinds of medicines. I believed in my heart to start trusting God to heal me from all of my illnesses and diseases. I've learned to believe Him as time went on and I grew in the Lord. He continues to be my physician today.

Neck Injury:

I was driving to church one afternoon when I was hit by another vehicle and sustained an injury to my neck that required a medical leave from work. I wanted to return to work but the doctor refused. I started praying, "Jesus I am bored, please let me go." Jesus said, "go back to work and no one will be able to tell that you were injured".

"For I will restore health unto thee, and I will heal thee of thy wounds, saith the LORD;" (Jeremiah 30:17a)

Then I returned to the doctor and he released me to return to work since I insisted. I began feeling pain again and was reprimanded for returning to work too soon. I remember what Jesus said and promised me. I began telling myself to hold on to God's promise and began getting better dayby-day. Before I knew it, my pain had left. That evening my supervisor asked me to work over time. I jokingly laughed and told him that I was not well enough to work over-time because I was in pain. I confessed to having something that I didn't have. The pain immediately returned and my face became very pale, so my supervisor ordered me to go home. I remembered earlier God saying I would be fine and was determined to stand on it. I told my supervisor that I could not go home because of God's promise. Another supervisor was a Christian, so I asked her to pray for me. She insisted that I go home again. I began to rebuke the pain and spoke the word of faith. I called the devil a liar with the authority of the Holy Ghost. Instantly my pain departed.

"Then touched he their eyes, saying, According to your faith be it unto you." (Matthew 9:29)

I went back to my supervisor and told her what happened. She agreed that the devil is a liar and the father of all lies. It is important never to call illness or pain into existence. God taught me a very important lesson about joking around with untruth that day.

"But let your communication be, Yea, yea; Nay,nay: for whatsoever is more than   these cometh of evil." (Matthew 5:37).

Chapter 3

God's Powerful Weapons "Prayer And Fasting"

One Sunday morning, during service, I was lying down on the last pew in excruciating pain and barely able to walk. Suddenly God told me to walk to the front and receive prayer. Somehow I knew in my heart and in the Spirit that I was not going to be healed but since I heard God's voice I obeyed. As we read in

1 Samuel 15:22b. To obey is better than sacrifice.

I slowly made my way up to the front and as I began walking down the side isle, I noticed that people began standing up as I passed them. I witnessed the Spirit of God falling upon each person and wondered what the purpose of God was for sending me to the front.

"And it shall come to pass, if thou shalt hearken diligently unto the voice of the Lord thy God, to observe and to do all his commandments which I command thee this day, that the Lord thy God will set thee on high above all nations of the earth: And all these blessings shall come on thee, and overtake thee, if thou shalt hearken unto the voice of the Lord thy God." (Deuteronomy 28:1-2)

Elizabeth Das

I was attending my local church when this occurred, but thought about this particular day for some time. Afterwards when I went to visit a church in city of Upland. A Sister from our former Church was attending this church also. She saw my ad on my car where I offered math tutoring and wanted to hire me. One day while teaching her in my home, she told me, "Sister I remember the day when you were sick at our old church and you were walking up to the front to receive prayer. I have never experienced the presence of God like that before even though I have been baptized in Jesus Name and came to church for two years. The day you passed by, I felt the Spirit of God for the very first time and it was so strong. Do you remember the whole church was getting up as the Spirit fell on them as you passed?" I remembered that day well because I was still wondering why God sent me to the front when I could barely walk. I felt that God allowed her to cross my path again for a reason. Through her, God answered my question about that day.

I was glad that I heard God and obeyed His voice.

"For we walk by faith, not by sight:" (2 Corinthians 5:7)

After my injury in September 1999, I could no longer walk so I stayed in the bed constantly praying and fasting day and night, since I did not sleep for 48 hours. I prayed day and night thinking I'd rather keep God in my mind rather than feel the pain. I was constantly talking with God. We are vessels of honor or dishonor. When we pray, we fill our vessel with God's fresh oil by praying in the Holy Ghost.

We must use our time wisely and not allow the cares of life to keep us from having a spiritually intimate relationship with our Creator. The most powerful weapon against the devil and his army is prayer and fasting.

"But ye, beloved, building up yourselves on your most holy faith, praying in the Holy Ghost," (Jude Vs.20)

You defeat evil when you pray and have a consistent prayer life. Consistency is omnipotent. Fasting will heighten the power of the Holy Spirit and you will have authority over demons. The Name of Jesus is so powerful when you say the words, "In the Name of Jesus." Also remember The Precious "Blood of Jesus" is your weapon. Ask God to cover you with His Blood. The Word of God states:

*"And from Jesus Christ, who is the faithful witness, and the first begotten of the dead, and the prince of the kings of the earth. Unto him that loved us, and **washed us from our sins in his own blood.**"*
(Revelation 1:5)

*"In so much that they brought forth the sick into the streets, and laid them on beds and couches, that at the least the **shadow** of Peter passing by might overshadow some of them." (Acts 5:15)*

Chapter 4

God The Great Strategist

W ho can know the mind of God? In 1999, I was working the swing shift at the Post Office when I bent over to pick up an item and felt severe back pain. I looked for my supervisor but couldn't find her or anyone. I went home thinking that the pain would leave after praying before going to sleep. When I woke-up the next morning with the pain there, I called the Elder of the church who prayed for my healing. While praying, I heard the Lord telling me to call my employer at the post office to notify them of my injury. I was then instructed to notify my superintendent once I returned to work. When I returned to work, I was summoned to the office to fill out the injury report. I refused to see their doctor because I didn't believe in going to the doctor. I trusted in God. Regrettably, my back pain only became worse. My employer needed a doctor's certification to support that I had sustained an injury, to justify light duty. By this time, I was making several requests to be seen by their doctor but now they were not so inclined to send me. It was not until they saw some improvement when I walked that they thought I had recovered. Now they referred me to see their work injury doctor who later referred me to an orthopedic specialist. He confirmed that I had sustained a permanent back injury.

It made my employer very upset. I was so glad that I agreed to see their doctor this time. I didn't know what the future held for me, but God did. Not only was I given light duty at work, but now they were aware that I had a serious disability. As my condition became worse, I was allowed only six hours of work, then four, and then two. My pain became so unbearable that the drive to work made it difficult to commute back and forth. I knew that I had to depend on God to heal me. I prayed and asked God what was His plan for me? He answered, *"You are going home."* I thought, surely they will call me to the office and send me home. I was later called into the office and sent home just like the Lord had spoken. As time progressed, my condition became worse and I required support to walk. A physician, who recognized the seriousness of my injury, recommended that I see a Worker's Compensation doctor who would take on my case.

One Friday evening as I opened the door while leaving the post office, I heard a voice of God saying, *"You are never coming back to this place again."* I was so amazed by the words that I began thinking perhaps I might be paralyzed or even fired. The voice was very clear and powerful. I knew without a doubt that it would come to pass, and I would not look back to this place where I had worked for 19 years. How things would work out financially for me was uncertain. However, God sees things from a distance as He was yet placing another step directing the way that I should go..

God was slowly and skillfully laying the foundation for my future like a master strategist for a time when I would no longer work for anyone else, but Him. After the weekend, I had found a new orthopedic physician who examined me. He placed me on temporary disability for almost a year. The post office sent me to be evaluated by one of their doctors and his opinion was contrary to that of my doctor. He said that I was fine and could pick up to 100 lbs. I couldn't even walk, stand or even sit very long, let alone pick up weight equivalent to my own frail body. My doctor was very upset. He disagreed with the other doctor's assessment of my health and physical abilities. Thank God that my doctor disputed this on my behalf and against my employer's doctor. My employer then referred the matter to a third doctor who would act as a mediating "referee." This referee was an orthopedic surgeon who later diagnosed me as being disabled. It wasn't because of the injury at work but because of my blood disease. So now everything took a different turn. I was born with this disease. I did not know anything about disability retirement. I prayed about this situation with anger in my heart. I know his job was to do what was fair to the patient and not to the employer. And in a vision I saw this doctor totally insane.

I immediately asked Jesus to forgive him. The Lord began to speak to me saying that the doctor had done his best for your benefit. I asked the Lord to show me because I could not see it that way; however, my answer would come later. Meanwhile, I applied for Permanent Disability Benefits because I could no longer work. I was uncertain whether my request would be approved. My employer and my doctor both knew that I not only had a back injury but three tumors on my lower back and Hemongioma in the spine. I had degenerative disk disease and a blood disease. My body was deteriorating rapidly and most painfully.

The painful symptoms of my diseases and injuries had taken a severe toll on me. I found myself unable to walk even with the supportive assistance. It was unknown what was causing the paralyses that afflicted my legs, so I was sent to get an MRI (Magnetic Resonance Imaging) of my head. The doctor was looking for any psychological condition. Who can know the mind of God and what steps He was taking for my future? God is the great strategist because little did I know then that all of this was for a reason. I just had to trust Him to take care of me. Permanent Disability Benefits can only be approved for individuals who have a personal medical condition that can be medically supported by a personal physician. Since my new doctor did not have any medical history, he refused to provide a complete medical assessment regarding my inability to work to the Department of Disability. I also found myself with the dilemma about my finances. I went to the only source I knew for the answers. The Lord said, "*You have many medical reports, send them all to the doctor.*"

Not only did I give the doctor all my medical reports, he was now ready to fill out my application for permanent disability retirement. Praise God! God is always ready to give an answer if we ask Him earnestly. It is important to always be still and listen for His response. Sometimes it does not come right away. I waited on the "Great Strategist" to arrange my life according to His will. The next few months were agonizing and challenging. Not only did I endure physical pain, but also I could no longer turn a page of a book. Since my dependency is on God for healing, I believed that I was going through this for a reason but surely I would not die. Believing this, I just thanked God every day for every moment that I was living and whatever condition I was in. I consumed myself in prayer and fasting to get through those times of agonizing pain. He was my only source of strength and my place of refuge in prayer.

My life had taken a big turn for the worse. I was no longer able to work in this debilitating state. With much prayer and supplication each day, my situation seemed to get worse, not better. Nevertheless, I knew God was the only answer. Without a doubt, I knew He would work things out for me. He had made His existence and presence known to me, and I knew He loved me. That was sufficient to hold on to and wait on the "Master Strategist," who had a definite plan for my life.

My mother, who was 85 years old, was living with me at the time. She was also disabled and needed assistance and care in her bed- ridden state. At a time when my loving mother needed me the most, I could not attend to her basic needs. Instead, my frail mother had to watch her daughter's health deteriorate in front of her. Two women, mother and daughter, in what seemed a hopeless situation, yet we both believed in the "Mighty God of Miracles." One day my mother saw me collapse on the floor. She screamed and cried out, helpless to do anything for me. This scene was so unbearable and horrifying for my mother to see me on the floor, but the Lord, in His mercy, raised me up from the floor. My brother, sister and family hearing about this were very concerned that my condition had reached to this extreme. My dear and elderly father, who was being taken care of elsewhere, would only cry and not say much, I prayed to the Lord for all of this to be over for all of our sakes. It was not just my personal pain and trial to endure; it was now affecting my loved ones. This was the darkest time of my life. I looked to God's promise from the beginning:

"When thou goest, thy steps shall not be straitened; and when thou runnest, thou shalt not stumble." (Proverbs 4:12)

With great joy in my heart, I thought about God's Word and promise. Not only would I be able to take a step, but have the ability to run one day. I dedicated more time to praying as there was not much else I could do but to pray and seek the face of God. It became an obsession day and night. The Word of God became my "Anchor of Hope" in a wavering sea. God provides our needs, so He made a way for me to obtain a motorized wheel chair that made life a little easier for me to move about. When I stood, I was unable to balance myself even with assistance. There was only discomfort and pain in my whole body and whatever comfort I had came from the "Comforter," the Holy Ghost. When God's people prayed over me, my body experienced temporary relief from pain, so I always sought for prayer from others. One day, I collapsed on the floor and was taken to the hospital. The doctor at the hospital tried to convince me to take pain medicine. He was persistent about this since he saw that my pain was extreme for many days. I finally gave into his instructions to take the medication but it was against what I believed.

For me, God was my healer and physician. I knew God had the ability to heal me at any time, just like He had done so many other times before, so why wouldn't He heal me now? I firmly believed that it was God's responsibility to help me. This is how I thought and prayed in faith and no one could change my thinking on this. I couldn't see it any other way so I waited on the "Master Strategist." My thought process was growing stronger by leaning on God. The more I prayed, the more my relationship with Him grew. It was so profound and personal that it cannot be explained to someone who does not know of the spiritual ways of God or of His very existence. He is an awesome God! The day I left the hospital, I called a friend to pick me up. She laid her hand over me to pray and I experienced temporary relief of pain. It was like taking God's prescription medicine. During this time, God sent a lady to pray with me every morning at 4.00 a.m. She would lay her hands on me and pray. I only experienced temporary relief and now I had been given a prayer partner. I believed with all my heart that God had everything under control.

Things got worse as my body continued to deteriorate. I was not getting enough blood supply or oxygen to my lower and upper extremities due to nerve damage. To add to my list of symptoms, I also became incontinent. I began to experience difficulty in pronouncing words due to spasms in my mouth. I had Sciatic Nerve damage and the list of symptoms kept growing.

My healing did not come quickly. I wondered what happened to His promise of Proverb 4:12. I thought maybe I had sinned. So I asked, "Lord Jesus, please let me know what I did wrong so I can repent." I asked God to talk to me or my friend, to send me a word. I was not angry at God, but I was asking Him with a humble heart. I was desperate for healing.

Later that day my phone rang, I thought to myself could this be my answer? But to my disappointment, the phone call was for someone else. I went to bed and awoke at 4 o'clock in the morning to pray. My prayer partner Sis. Rena came over to pray with me. I looked at her and wondered that may be God had spoken to her and she had my answer, but again to my disappointment, no answer came.

After she left, I went to my room to lie down and rest. As I lay there, at 9.00 am I heard the back door open; it was Carmen the house keeper. She entered she asked me *"how are you feeling?"* I said *"I feel awful."* Then I turned back and headed back to my room. Carmen said, *"I have a word for you."* While I was praying at church today, Jesus came to me and

39

said, "*Sis. Elizabeth Das is going through a trial, it is her fiery long trial, and she has done nothing wrong. She will come out as gold and I love her a lot.*" I know I was in the throne room with Him the night before when I was asking for an answer to my question.

Behold, the LORD'S hand is not shortened, that it cannot save; neither his ear heavy, that it cannot hear. (Isaiah 59:1)

At this point in my life I felt as though I would go insane. I could no longer read, remember nor concentrate normally. My only choice and reason for living was to worship God and pray exceedingly. I only slept short periods of approximately three to four hours every other day. When I slept, God was my Shalom. Glory and praise and honor to His Holy Name! I cried out to the Lord in my prayers, "God, I know I can come out of this instantly because I have faith that you can and will heal me". I began to think about my trial that maybe I could not come out of it on my faith alone. Trials have a beginning and an end.

A time to kill, and a time to heal; a time to break down, and a time to build up; (Ecclesiastes 3:3)

I had to believe that once this was all over, I would have a powerful testimony of faith that would stand forever. A testimony of faith that I would share to many as a witness of the Wonderful Works of an Almighty God! It would all be worth it, was what I kept repeating to myself. I had to believe in my "Anchor of Hope" because there wasn't any other way but **His Way**! And it was in **His way** that it came to pass that I would be led to the One who was endowed with the powerful gift of healing, given in His name. God's Word never changes, so God does not change either. He is the same yesterday, today and forever. As Born-Again Believers, we must profess our faith in love and love the Word of God.

"Being born again, not of corruptible seed, but of incorruptible, by the word of God, which liveth and abideth forever." (1 Peter 1:23)

Biblical men of God had their trials also. Why would it be any different today that God should not try us? I am not comparing myself to the godly men of the Holy Bible because I am far from comparison to the Holy disciples. If God tested the faith of men hundreds of years ago, then He will also test men and women of today.

*"Blessed is the man that endureth temptation: for when he is **tried**, he shall receive the crown of life, which the Lord hath promised to them that love him." (James 1:12)*

I thought about the biblical account of Daniel. He found himself in a situation where his faith was tried. God protected Daniel in the den of lions because he would not obey King Darius's law. He only prayed to God and refused to pray to King Darius. Then there was Job, a devote man who loved God, who lost all that he had and suffered disease in his body, yet Job would not curse God. There were so many other men and women mentioned in the Holy Bible. No matter what they went through, their trial had a beginning and an end. The Lord was with them through it all because they trusted in him. I hold on to the lessons of these biblical accounts that are given to us for example and inspiration. God is the answer to everything. Trust in Him only and stay true to His Word because His Word is true to you!

Holding faith, and a good conscience; which some having put away concerning faith have made shipwreck (1 Timothy 1:19)

When your faith is tried, remember to stand on the Word of God. In every attack from the enemy, the battle can be won through the Power of His Word.

The LORD is my strength and song, and he is become my salvation: he is my God, (Ex. 15:2a)

The God of my rock; in him will I trust: he is my shield, and the horn of my salvation, my high tower, and my refuge, my saviour; thou savest me from violence (2Sam. 22:3)

The LORD is my rock, and my fortress, and my deliverer; my God, my strength, in whom I will trust; my buckler, and the horn of my salvation, and my high tower. (Psa. 18:2)

The LORD is my light and my salvation; whom shall I fear? the LORD is the strength of my life; of whom shall I be afraid? (Psa. 27:1)

In God have I put my trust: I will not be afraid what man can do unto me. (Psa. 56:11)

In God is my salvation and my glory: the rock of my strength, and my refuge, is in God. (Psa. 62:7)

Chapter 5

Speaking Out Your Faith

I had a dust allergy for some time that made my face itch. I believed that God would heal me of this condition. One day a co-worker looked at me saying that my allergy was very bad. I told her I did not have the allergy, explaining that I believed that God was already taking care of my petition for healing. This was my "don't name-it", and "don't claim it" belief. The Lord honored my petition that very day by removing the condition and all symptoms. What a wonderful God we serve! We do not have to confess with our mouth and give names to our symptoms. When you receive prayer, believe that it has already been taken care of it in heaven and that an Angel has been sent forth to bring you your healing. Speak your faith into existence, not your sickness and diseases. I bring to mind the biblical story of Jesus and the Centurion at Capernaum:

"And when Jesus was entered into Capernaum, there came unto him a centurion, beseeching him, and saying, Lord, my servant lieth at home sick of the palsy, grievously tormented. And Jesus saith unto him, I will come and heal him. The centurion answered and said, Lord, I am not worthy that thou shouldest come under my roof: but speak the word only, and my servant shall be healed. For I am a man under authority, having soldiers under me: and I say to this man, Go, and he goeth; and to another, Come, and he cometh; and to my servant, Do this, and he doeth it. When Jesus heard it, he marveled, and said to them that followed, Verily I say unto you, I have not found so great faith, no, not in Israel." (Mathew 8:5-10)

The Centurion came humbly to the Lord believing in the power of the words of Jesus. The Centurion's own words revealed to Jesus about his faith in the power of the "spoken Word" that would heal his servant. We can bring faith and hope to others by what we say to them. We must allow the Holy Ghost to speak through our mouth when we have an opportunity to witness to others.

This is His Way of using us to effectively touch the lives of others and plant the seed of Salvation. In times such as these, God will give us the words to speak, with anointing, because He knows our heart and our desire to reach out to the sinner. I am so thankful for God's Love, Mercy, and Grace that leads us to repentance. He is ready to forgive us of our sins and knows our weaknesses for He knows that we are human.

"And he said unto me, My grace is sufficient for thee: for my strength is made perfect in weakness. Most gladly therefore will I rather glory in my infirmities, that the power of Christ may rest upon me. Therefore I take pleasure in infirmities, in reproaches, in necessities, in persecutions, in distresses for Christ's sake: for when I am weak, then am I strong." (2 Corinthians 12:9-10)

And Jesus said unto them, Because of your unbelief: for verily I say unto you, If ye have faith as a grain of mustard seed, ye shall say unto this mountain, Remove hence to yonder place; and it shall remove; and nothing shall be impossible unto you. (Matthew 17:20)

That evening the skin allergy was completely cured since I did not accept the package of satan.

Chapter 6

The Healing Power Of God And His Servant

I want to begin this chapter by first telling you a little about Brother James Min. Brother James had a shoe repair shop in Diamond Bar, California where he also witnessed to his customers about the power of God. At one time, he was an atheist, but came to accept the Christian belief. He later came to know the Apostles' doctrine of truth and is now a strong believer baptized in the Name of Jesus and has received the Holy Ghost with the evidence of speaking in other languages or tongues. When I first met Brother James, he told me about his testimony and how he prayed asking God to use him in the gifts, so that others would believe and come to know God through miracles.

As Christians, we need to operate in the gifts and not be afraid to ask God to use us. These gifts are also for us today. The early church of the New Testament was sensitive to the Spirit of God and ministered in the Gifts of the Spirit.

Jesus said:

*"Verily, verily, I say unto you, He that believeth on me, the works that I do shall he do also; and **greater works** than these shall he do; because I go unto my Father". (John 14:12)*

Pray that your church leader will help you to understand these gifts and will be supportive of your gift. Ask God to help you use them because it comes directly from God. Don't be high- minded if your gift is one that operates openly in the church. With some gifts, God will use you as a vessel to get what He wants done. You may have several gifts and may not know it. Some gifts will not make you very popular but you will have to obey God when He speaks. It all depends on the gift. Pray for wisdom to use your gift under His anointing power. God chose you for a reason and He does not make mistakes. Gifts are for the edification of the church.

There is only one true church which worships Him in spirit and in truth.

"Now there are diversities of gifts, but the same Spirit. And there are differences of administrations, but the same Lord. And there are diversities of operations, but it is the same God which worketh all in all. But the manifestation of the Spirit is given to every man to profit withal. For to one is given by the Spirit the word of wisdom; to another the word of knowledge by the same Spirit; To another faith by the same Spirit; to another the gifts of healing by the same Spirit; To another the working of miracles; to another prophecy; to another discerning of spirits; to another divers kinds of tongues; to another the interpretation of tongues: But all these worketh that one and the selfsame Spirit, dividing to every man severally as he will." (I Corinthians 12:4-11)

Brother James told me that he prayed for these gifts in order to operate in the Holy Ghost with signs of miracles of God's wonderful works. He read the Bible day and night continuously. He realized that through the operation of the Gifts of the Spirit, the seed of faith would be planted in the heart of the unbeliever. We must be an example of our faith, as Jesus himself said, that believers themselves would perform these miracles and much more.

"Now faith is the substance of things hoped for, the evidence of things not seen." (Hebrews 11:1)

" But without faith it is impossible to please him: for he that cometh to God must believe that he is, and that he is a rewarder of them that diligently seek him". (Hebrews 11:6)

Brother James had a vision that God would give him spiritual gifts. Today he operates through the gifts of Healing and Deliverance. It was through the ministry of Brother James that the appointed time was set in heaven the day I would walk again, free from any assistance. Brother James is not a pastor or minister of a church. He does not hold any high position in a church although he has been offered positions and money because of the spiritual gifts. He is humbled by the gift that God has entrusted him with. I have seen how God uses him to cast out demons from people in the Name of Jesus and healing comes to the sick. Demons are under God's authority in the name of Jesus when Brother James calls them out. He will ask the demons questions in Jesus Name and they will respond to Brother James. I have seen this personally many times; especially when he asked demons to confess who the real God is. The demon will reply, "Jesus". But for them it is too late to turn to Jesus. I learned a lot about the spiritual world by going through this trial and leaning on God for healing.

"And he said unto them, Go ye into all the world, and preach the gospel to every creature. He that believeth and is baptized shall be saved; but he that believeth not shall be damned. And these signs shall follow them that believe; In my name shall they cast out devils; they shall speak with new tongues; They shall take up serpents; and if they drink any deadly thing, it shall not hurt them; they shall lay hands on the sick, and they shall recover." (Mark 16:15-18)

By the grace of God, Brother James is ready to witness to anyone at any time about Jesus. He operates in the healing and deliverance ministry at home meetings or at churches where he has been invited. Brother James quotes from the Bible:

Nevertheless, brethren, I have written the more boldly unto you in some sort, as putting you in mind, because of the grace that is given to me of God, That I should be the minister of Jesus Christ to the Gentiles, ministering the gospel of God, that the offering up of the Gentiles might be acceptable, being sanctified by the Holy Ghost. I have therefore whereof I may glory through Jesus Christ in those things which pertain to God. For I will not dare to speak of any of those things which Christ hath not wrought by me, to make the Gentiles obedient, by word and deed, Through mighty signs and wonders, by the power of the Spirit of God; so that from Jerusalem, and round about unto Illyricum, I have fully preached the gospel of Christ. (Roman 15:15-19)

The day I met him, Brother James asked me a few questions about my health. I told him everything and my symptoms. I also showed him where I had three tumors. The tumors are on the outside of my spine, and the other was on the inside of the spine. Brother James checked my spine and explained that my spine was not straight inline from the middle. He checked my legs by comparing them side-by-side and showed me that one leg was almost 3 inches shorter than the other. One hand was also shorter than the other. He prayed for my spine and it came back to its original place where he could run his finger straight inline parallel to my spine. He prayed for my leg and it began to move in front of my eyes, then it stopped growing when it was even with the other leg. The same happened with my hand. It grew evenly to the other hand. Brother James then asked me to put away my walking support and ordered me to stand up and walk in the Name of Jesus. I did as he asked and began to walk miraculously. Witnessing this, my friend came running yelling, "Liz hold on to me, hold on to your support or you will fall!" I knew I had the strength to walk that very moment and took that step in faith. I was so elated with joy!

I had muscular weakness in my legs due to the lack of exercise from being unable to walk for such a long time. It took a while to get my muscles back into shape; even today I do not have the full strength of my muscles. Thank God, I am walking and driving my car. No one can tell me that God doesn't perform miracles today. Nothing is impossible with God. With overwhelming joy, I went to visit the doctor who knew of my disability. Immediately as I walked into the office, free from any assistance, cane or wheelchair, the medical staff was totally amazed. The nurses rushed to get the doctor who was also unbelievably surprised that he even took x- rays. What he saw was that the tumors were still there, but for some mysterious reason, I was able to walk in spite of this. Praise God! I believe that these tumors will also be gone soon!

The day God healed me, I began telling everyone that God is our healer and His plan of salvation is for those who believe and will follow Him. Thank God for Brother James and for all of God's benefits!

My first part of the promise had come to pass.

> *"When thou goest, thy steps shall not be straitened; and when thou runnest, thou shalt not stumble." (Proverb 4:12)*

Many times I thought I would fall, but I never did

> *"Bless the LORD, O my soul, and forget not all his benefits: Who forgiveth all thine iniquities; who healeth all thy diseases; Who redeemeth thy life from destruction; who crowneth thee with lovingkindness and tender mercies; Who satisfieth thy mouth with good things; so that thy youth is renewed like the eagle's." (Psalms 103:2-5).*

Chapter 7

Not Giving Way To The Devil Or The Things Of The Devil

M y friend Rose from California called me early one morning. She told me that the previous night her husband Raul had gone to bed while she remained in the guest room listening to a popular late night radio talk show regarding the Ouija board. The lights were out and the room was dark. Suddenly she said she felt a presence in the room. She looked towards the doorway and there was a man standing looking somewhat like her husband. This figure quickly moved like a flash and pinned her down flat onto the bed where she was. This "thing" then pulled her up by her arms into a sitting position facing him eye to eye. She could clearly see that there were no eyes in the sockets but just deep hollow blackness. The arms that still held her up were grayish in color like death and his veins protruded from the skin. She realized immediately that this was not her husband but an unclean fallen angel.

As you know a demon and a fallen angel have completely different characteristics. Fallen angels were thrown out of heaven with Lucifer, they have completely different jobs. Fallen angels can move things around just like humans, but a demon needs a human body of to operate its plan. Demons are the spirits of people who have died without Jesus; they also have limited power.

And there appeared another wonder in heaven; and behold a great red dragon, having seven heads and ten horns, and seven crowns upon his heads. And his tail drew the third part of the stars of heaven, and did cast them to the earth: and the dragon stood before the woman which was ready to be delivered, for to devour her child as soon as it was born. (Revelation 12:3,4)

Rose was still defenseless and unable to speak in a frozen state. She said she attempted to call out to Raul but could only make short struggling sounds as if someone was tightening her vocal cords. She could still hear the radio host in the background and knew she was not asleep as her eyes were fully open and repeated to herself not to close them. Earlier she remembered closing her eyes briefly before this incident occurred and saw a vision or dream of large claw marks ripping through wallpaper.

I have known Rose for almost 30 years. Rose left the church approximately 10 years and was no longer walking with the Lord. We always kept in contact and I continued to pray for her to return to God. Rose told me that she had been speaking in tongues very powerfully for no apparent reason while driving home from work at least several times. She felt this was very unusual because she was not praying at all. She realized that God was dealing with her through the Holy Spirit. His love was reaching out to her, and she knew God was in control because He chose the time of His visitations. Rose said she closed her eyes and her mind and screamed, "JESUS!" In a flash the fallen angel jumped off her body and walked away without touching the ground.

She remained motionless until she could move again. She awoke Raul, who said it was just a bad dream. He placed her in bed beside him and quickly fell asleep. Rose began to cry and thought about the horror that had just occurred and noticed that she was in a fetal position. Suddenly she began speaking in tongues as the supernatural power of the Holy

Ghost came over her and led her back into that dark room. She shut the door behind her realizing exactly what she needed to do. She began to worship God loudly and exalted His Name until she fell to the floor feeling exhausted but with great peace.

When she opened the door, to her amazement, Raul was standing in the living room with all the lights on. She walked directly to their bed and slept with an awesome peace. Next evening while preparing dinner, Raul asked Rose if that "thing" from the night before would return. Surprised at his question, Rose asked why he would ask this because he did not even believe it had happened. Raul told Rose that after she went into the room to pray, something came after him. This is why he was up with all the lights on. After she had prayed and went to sleep, he was attacked by something awful that kept him awake until 4:00 the following morning. He used Om humming meditation struggling from 11:00 pm until morning. Rose remembered that Raul had a Ouija board in the hallway closet that he refused to get rid of when she first moved into the house. She told Raul that she did not know whether it would return, but he should get rid of the Ouija board. Raul quickly threw it into the trashcan outside. Rose said that it took that horrible incident to make him get rid of it!

When Rose called me, I told her that the fallen angel could still be inside the house, so we needed to pray over the phone together. Rose got the olive oil to anoint the house with me on speakerphone. When I said the word "ready" I told her that she would begin speaking in tongues in the Holy Ghost instantly. When I said "ready", Rose began speaking in tongues instantly and put the phone down to anoint. I could hear her voice fading away as she prayed throughout the house, anointing doors and windows in the Name of Jesus. Rose was now out of my hearing range when something told me to tell her to go into the garage. At that same moment, Rose said she was anointing rooms and was at the back door leading into the garage. She felt an evil presence behind the door when she anointed it. Believing in God's protection, Rose said she opened it and walked into the very dark garage. The power of the Holy

Ghost got stronger as she entered and could feel it was there! She walked towards another door leading out to a patio where the trashcan was located. It was the same trashcan where Raul had disposed of the Ouija board the day before. Without hesitation, Rose said she poured olive oil over the Ouija board as she prayed loudly and with fervor in the Holy Ghost, then she closed the lid. She made her way back to the living room and could hear my voice calling out to her "go into the garage because it is in there". Rose told me that she had already taken care of "it." This confirmed that evil was in the garage while we prayed.

Rose said it all made sense to her now. God in His tender mercy and loving kindness was preparing Rose for this very day, even though she was not serving Him. According to Rose, this experience is what brought her back to God with a commitment like she has never felt before. She now attends Apostolic Lighthouse in Norwalk, California. She was so grateful to God for His love and protection. God made her ready to face the fallen angel of that night with the undeniable spiritual armor of the Holy Ghost. For Rose what happened was the supernatural manifestation of the power of God in the Name of Jesus. It was His love for Rose to return to His ways. Believe that His hand is not too short to save or to deliver, even concerning those who oppose themselves who choose not to believe in what they cannot see or feel. Our Redeemer paid the price for us at the cross with His Blood. He will never force anyone to love Him. God's Word tells us that you must come as a little child and promises that if you seek Him with all your heart, you will find Him. Unbelievers and skeptics cannot change what is and what is to come. Thirst for the righteousness of God and drink of the Living Water of Life.

"Wherefore, when I came, was there no man? When I called, was there none to answer? Is my hand shortened at all, that it cannot redeem? or have I no power to deliver? Behold, at my rebuke I dry up the sea, I make the rivers a wilderness: their fish stinketh, because there is no water, and dieth for thirst." (Isaiah 50:2)

"In meekness instructing those that oppose themselves; if God peradventure will give them repentance to the acknowledging of the

truth; And that they may recover themselves out of the snare of the devil, who are taken captive by him at his will." (2 Timothy 2:25-26)

Chapter 8

Dream And Vision – The "Warning"

O ne morning I had a dream of impending danger happening while I was driving my car. In this dream the front tire burst with a loud sound. It was so loud that it woke me up. It was so real that the dream felt as though I were awake or somewhere in between. I prayed about this during the week and decided to take my car to get the tires checked. Unfortunately, my plans were interrupted and I didn't take care of it. That same week some friends and I went to pray for an Indian family that was in need of prayer. On our way to their house the tire of my car burst on the freeway by the cemetery. Instantly I remembered the dream just like I saw it. Here we were, in my car with a flat tire with the family insisting that we come to their home. After the tire was repaired we returned to get another vehicle and continued to see the family. The family had a situation with their only son who was involved in a legal matter and would face time in prison. They were worried that he would also be deported to their native country. The young man's mother called me earlier that day crying and explained the charges he would be facing. Thinking of the worse case scenario, she was certain that he would be found guilty and then deported never to see her son again. She said she could not work because she would cry constantly in front of her patients.

As she wept, I began to pray for the situation over the phone with her. I began to speak in the Holy Ghost in an unknown language or tongues as the Spirit of God moved. I prayed until she said that her heart was no longer burdened and she felt comforted.

"Likewise the Spirit also helpeth our infirmities: for we know not what we should pray for as we ought, but the Spirit itself maketh intercession for us with groanings which cannot be uttered And he that searcheth the hearts knoweth what is the mind of the Spirit because he maketh intercession for the saints according to the will of God."
(Romans 8:26- 27).

The mother asked if she could call me before she went to his trial the next morning. I told her yes, and that I would pray for God to intervene. I asked her to call me after court, because I wanted to know what kind of miracle God performed. The next day the young man's mother called me with much joy saying, *"You would not believe what happened?"* I said, *"I will believe because that is the kind of God we serve"*! She continued to say that they did not have any record on my son. The lawyer said the court found no such name or any charges against him although she and the lawyer had proof of paper work in their hand.

God had answered our prayers. Her faith was so lifted that from that day forward she accepted what a mighty God we serve and how God takes care of things if we bring them before him in prayer with all our heart. She became a witness of the working miracles of God and gave testimony to what the Lord had done for them. As for the flat tire, that was only a small setback that should not have happened had I taken care of it beforehand. Nevertheless, the Lord made a way for us to reach this family due to their persistence that we come and pray with them. We always have to be ready to counter-attack those forces that keep us from doing the will of God. We have to go against every plan of the enemy, our adversary, the devil, through perseverance especially when we see those obstacles in the way.

When we arrived at the family's home, I remember we prayed and witnessed to the whole family. We thoroughly enjoyed a wonderful time of preaching and teaching the Word of God. That day, the joy of the Lord was and continues to be our strength! He will bless those who do His will.

Chapter 9

The All Night Prayer Meeting

One night some friends and I decided to pray all night. We then agreed that we would pray once a month in our "All Night Prayer Meeting". We have wonderful experiences during these all night prayer meetings. Our unified home prayer time became so powerful that immediately those who later joined us felt the difference in their own prayers. It was no longer a religious routine but praying in the Holy Ghost with manifestations of the Gifts of the Spirit. As we prayed, some began to experience what it was to be wrestling with the devil. Forces were coming against us as we reached a higher level in our prayers that lead us through spiritual battlefields. We were at war with the devil and began calling fasting days. We had tapped into something that was spiritually powerful that compelled us to seek God even more. During one such prayer meeting at 3:30 a.m., my friend Karen got up to get the anointing oil. She began putting oil on my hands and feet and then began to prophesy saying that I have to go to many places to take the Word of God and that God would use me for His purpose. At first I was very upset with Karen because this was not possible and it did not make any sense. At that time in my life, I had not gone anywhere for nearly 10 years because I couldn't walk. My leg muscles were still weak and I had those painful tumors pressing against my spine. I pondered on

Karen's words, and then God spoke to me, saying, "I am the Lord speaking to you" through her mouth, I then understood that it was not just Karen's enthusiasm speaking to me. I was sorry and asked God to forgive me for my thought.

A few days later I received a call from someone in Chicago, Illinois who needed spiritual help, so we decided to go to Chicago the following week. That was a great miracle in itself because I hadn't thought about venturing out at that time. Because of the prophetic message, I made the trip to Chicago on pure faith. Without the prophetic message, I would have definitely not gone. That week my physical health got worse and I couldn't get out of bed. I also heard that it had snowed considerably in Chicago. I realized that my faith was being tried. During that time in my life, I needed a wheelchair to get around. The family in Chicago was experiencing demonic forces coming against them. They had recently turned to God and stopped practicing witchcraft. Many of their family members had also turned to our Lord Jesus Christ. The Lord had healed and delivered them from these demonic forces that held them bondage to sin. I realized that God would have to give me the stamina to endure such a trip and it quickly became evident that it was God's will for me to go. I had experienced two dreams where God was telling me that I must obey His voice. I did not disobey God and had learned not to question Him. I was learning quickly that His ways did not have to make any sense to me. The day we arrived in Chicago the weather was hot. I was also pain-free. We walk by faith and not by sight as the Scripture says. When things look impossible to us, we must believe that "All things are possible with God". He took care of everything and gave me the energy to do His will in Chicago. We also had time to visit and minister to other families in their homes.

Departing for home the thunderstorm started, many flights were cancelled, but thank God although our flight was late we were able to return back to California. Praise God! He is truly my "Rock and Shield" my protector from the spiritual and natural storms. This trip was a testimony of faith and blessings to all of us. Had I not obeyed, I would not have experienced the blessings of the work of God's Hands. God never ceases to amaze me with how He speaks to us today. The Almighty God, still speaking to ordinary people like me. What a privilege to serve our Creator and see His mighty works, touching the lives of people today who believe and call on Him. It took a prophesied message and two dreams before God got my full attention. I am reminded that we do not fully understand the thoughts of God and what plans He may have for someone. In that moment, we must obey even though it may not make any sense or have reason to us. In time I learnt to hear His voice and discern the spirits. He will never tell you to do something that is against His Word. Obedience is better than sacrifice.

"And Samuel said, Hath the LORD as great delight in burnt offerings and sacrifices, as in obeying the voice of the LORD? Behold, to obey is better than sacrifice, and to hearken than the fat of rams."
(1 Samuel 15:22)

"For my thoughts are not your thoughts, neither are your ways my ways, saith the LORD. For as the heavens are higher than the earth, so are my ways higher than your ways, and my thoughts than your thoughts." (Isaiah 55: 8, 9)

Chapter 10.

The Prophetic Message

I t is a blessing to have friends who share the same common belief and love for God. I have a friend Karen who was once a co-worker when I worked at the U.S. Post Office. Karen came to know the Lord when I witnessed to her. She later accepted the early church apostolic doctrine of truth. Karen is a kind person with a heart for giving to the missionary work in Mumbai, India. She had a heart-felt love for the ministry there and donated her own money for the building of a church in Mumbai.

One day when I was living in West Covina, Karen brought her friend Angela to my home. Her friend was so excited and on fire for God. She told me her testimony about past attempts to commit suicide by cutting herself multiple times and her past with prostitution. I loved her sweet spirit and asked her if she did not mind praying for me. "*Here*"? She asked. "*Yes here*", I answered back. As she began praying for me, the Spirit of Prophecy came over her. She began to speak the Word of the Lord, "*God is telling you to finish the book that you have started. It is going to be a blessing to many people. Through this book many people will be saved.*" I was so happy because neither she nor Karen had any idea that I had started writing my memories years ago. I was first inspired to write this book a year ago by Mrs. Saroj Das and a friend. One day, a sister in the Lord from a local Church, came to me with a pen in her hand ordering me to, *"Write now!"*

I started to write until I experienced more problems with my health and then stopped because it was too big a task for me to accomplish. Now, the matter of the book had resurfaced. No one had known about my attempt to write a book. My experiences would be collected and written, so others would receive inspiration. I had to obey but how it would all happen was still a big mystery to me. I couldn't physically write it for many reasons, but again, God would have to find a way to make it happen. I had the desire and the urgency to do it after hearing the message; however, God would have to do the rest. My initial journey was to find the Living God and He found me! If I do not write about my experiences with God, these true accounts will be forever lost. So many people's lives have been affected and marvelously touched, that this book could not contain every incident and miracle. God's miracles will continue even when I am absent from this body and present with the Lord. Faith begins somewhere. It has a beginning and is limitless because there are different measures of faith. When Faith is planted it is watered by the Word of God and fed through the testimonies of others. I thought about the scripture that says that if we have faith as a mustard seed we can move mountains. How could I have known that this journey to America would take me through a maze of life changing experiences or that I would one day write about honoring His ways? One day I mentioned to my friend Rose about God's message and His plan about this Book. Rose listened and looked at my notes. She had known me for years and already knew a lot about my life in America. The writing took a form of its own that could not be imagined by two inexperienced individuals. The Lord made a way and through many difficulties and very "strange" occurrences, the book would be completed. The Lord had spoken and now His plan is fulfilled.

Karen's friend continued to prophesy. She told me, *"God is going to do something for you by the end of this month."* And many other things God spoke to me through her prophesied messages. I began to recall how I went through so many hardships for this truth. The day God spoke to me through this young lady, God answered the question of my heart. I was to do His will and the words of encouragement proceeded forth. Words I needed to hear. She prophesied that I was a "*Vessel of Gold*". I was so humbled by this. By faith, we do our best to walk in harmony with God and with uncertainty, if we are really pleasing Him. That day He blessed me by letting me know that I was pleasing Him. My heart was filled with great joy. Sometimes we forget what we ask for but when our prayer is answered we are surprised.

We must believe that He is no respecter of persons as the Bible says. It does not matter what your status or your cast is, because with God, there is no cast or status system in life. God loves us all the same and wants us to have a personal relationship with Him; not the religious traditions passed on by many generations that have served idols and man. Idols cannot see and cannot hear. Religion cannot change your life or heart. Religion only makes you feel good temporarily because of its self-gratification. The true God is waiting to embrace and receive you. Jesus was the sacrificial Lamb of God slain before the world. When He died at the cross, He rose again and lives today and forever. Now we can have direct communion with God through Jesus Christ our Lord and Savior. There are different levels in our walk with God. We must desire more of Him and continue to grow in love, faith, and trust. I was very humbled by this experience. My whole desire and purpose is to please Him. There are spiritual growth levels of maturity in God. You mature in time, but it all depends on the time and effort you put into your relationship with Him. By the end of the month circumstances led me to leave the church that I had attended for 23 years. God closed one door and opened another. He has been closing and opening doors ever since just like the stepping stones that I first mentioned in the beginning of this book. God was taking care of me all the time. I briefly attended a church in West Covina then another door flung wide open.

That same young lady prophesied again a few years later and told me to pack, *"you are moving"*. I was very surprised because my mom was so elderly and my condition still had not improved. I believed the Lord. One year later it happened, I did move from California to Texas. Places where I had never been to, nor did I know anyone. This was the beginning of yet another adventure in my life's journey. As a single lady, I was in submission to God's Voice and had to obey. God never took anything away from me. He just replaced things and places and kept bringing new friendships and people into my life. Thank you Lord, my life today is so blessed!

Chapter 11

A Move of Faith

I n April 2005, I moved to the Longhorn state of Texas. God was using different people through prophetic messages. The move was confirmed and all I had to do was take that leap of faith. It first started back in 2004 when Brother James and Angela, a friend in the Lord, were praying with me over the telephone. Sister Angela began to prophesy by telling me, *"You are going to move by the end of this year."* From January through August of that year nothing happened, and then in September, one afternoon my mom called me to her bedroom. She told me that my sister's family is moving to another state and they wanted me to move with them. The decision where to move was not made but the options were Texas, Arizona, or leave America altogether and move to Canada. I then called Sister Angela and told her what had happened. I told her that I definitely did not want to go to Texas. It had never occurred to me to ever go there, so it was not an option to even live there. To my disappointment, Sister Angela said Texas is the state. Out of obedience it was settled and this is what made us eventually move to Texas. Little did I know at that time, that God's stepping-stones had already been laid in that direction. After my conversation with Sister Angela, I made airline reservations for myself to be in Texas in two weeks. Unknown to me, my sister's family had already been to Texas to see the area around Plano.

Sister Angela was praying over me and told me do not worry, Jesus is going to pick you up from the airport. Brother and Sister Blakey were so kind and patient that it reminded me of the prophecy of Sister Angela. They gladly picked me up at the airport and assisted me with all my needs in such a loving and caring way.

Sister Angela continued to say that the first house I will see I would love it, but it would not be my house. Through the Internet I began calling United Pentecostal Churches in that area and contacted Pastor Conkle who is the Pastor of the United Pentecostal Church in the City of Allen, Texas. I explained to Pastor Conkle what I was doing in Texas. Afterwards he asked me to call Nancy Conkle. I was not sure why and thought that maybe she was his wife or secretary. It turned out that Nancy Conkle is the matriarch of the family, a nurturing mother of the family and of the church. Sister Conckle had raised her own six children and helped in raising her brothers and sisters which totaled eleven siblings! After speaking with Nancy Conkle, I realized why Pastor Conkle had me speak with this strong and caring lady who made me feel instantly welcomed. Sister Conkle then connected me to her other brother, James Blakey, who is a realtor and his wife Alice Blakey. They live in the small town of Wylie, Texas, just a few minutes from Allen through the backcountry roads of the flat lands.

After becoming familiar with the area, I flew back to California to put my house on the market. My home sold in two months. I then flew back to Texas to begin house hunting. I prayed about which city God wanted me to live in because there were so many little cities and towns. God said "Wylie." It is important to pray and ask God for His will before making important decisions because it will always be the right one.

"For it is better, if the will of God be so, that you suffer for well doing, than for evil doing." (1 Peter 3:17)

I later explained to Brother and Sister Blakey about the prophesied messages and that I wanted to obey God. They were very careful to respect my wishes and listened to everything that I told them that God had spoken to me. I also told them that during my first trip to Texas, God said, *"You do not know what I have for you."* They were so patient with me that I will always be most grateful for their sensitivity to the things of God. The Blakey Family played a big part in the fulfillment of this prophetic message and my new life in Texas. We began seeing houses in Wylie for three days, and on the third day I had to return to California in the evening. They took me to see a model home in a new tract and then Sister Blakey said, "This is your house." I immediately knew that it truly was. Quickly I began the paperwork for the purchase, then immediately left to the airport, knowing things would somehow get done. At that same time, God told me to go to India for three months. I did not question Him, so I gave power of attorney to Brother Blakey to continue with the purchase of the house in Texas, and I gave power of attorney to my nephew Steve who is in real estate to take care of my finances in California. I was returning to my native country India, after ten years. Thank God for my healing because I could not have done it without mobility to my legs. I was flying to India and buying a home in Texas. Things were changing rapidly in my life.

Return to India.

When I arrived in India I quickly noticed that things had changed in a relatively short time. For 25 years I prayed and fasted for this country to have a Revival. India is a very religious country of idolatry, the worship of statues of stone and wood and of iron. Religious images that cannot see, speak, or hear and have no power at all. They are religious traditions that do not bring change to the mind or to the heart.

"And I will utter my judgments against them touching all their wickedness, who have forsaken me, and have burned incense unto other gods, and worshipped the works of their own hands."
(Jeremiah 1:16)

Christianity was the minority in this country where there was so much persecution and hatred between religions and especially against Christians. The oppression against Christians only made them stronger in their faith through the spilling of innocent blood, churches being burned, people beaten, or killed. Sadly, mothers and fathers rejected their own children if they turned to Jesus and left their family religion. Outcasts maybe, but not fatherless as God is our Heavenly Father who will wipe the tears from our eyes.

"Suppose ye that I am come to give peace on earth? I tell you, Nay; but rather division: For from henceforth there shall be five in one house divided, three against two, and two against three. The father shall be divided against the son, and the son against the father; the mother against the daughter, and the daughter against the mother; the mother in law against her daughter in law, and the daughter in law against her mother in law." (Luke 12:51-53)

I was so surprised to see people everywhere who were walking with Bibles and I heard of prayer meetings. There were many oneness churches and believers in one God. God came to live among us in the flesh, in the body of Jesus Christ. And so is the mystery of godliness of the one true God.

*"And without controversy great is the mystery of godliness: **God was manifest in the flesh**, justified in the Spirit, seen of angels, preached unto the Gentiles, believed on in the world, received up into glory." (1 Timothy 3:16)*

"Philip saith unto him, Lord, shew us the Father, and it sufficeth us. Jesus saith unto him, Have I been so long time with you, and yet hast thou not known me, Philip? He that hath seen me hath seen the Father; and how sayest thou then, Shew us the Father? Believest thou not that I am in the Father, and the Father in me? The words that I speak unto you I speak not of myself: but the Father that dwelleth in me, he doeth the works. Believe me that I am in the Father, and the Father in me: or else believe me for the very works' sake." (John 14:8-11)

Elizabeth Das

> *"Thou believest that there is one God; thou doest well: the devils*
> *also believe, and tremble." (James 2:19)*

It was such a joy to see people thirsty for God. Their worship was so powerful. It was a completely different India than the one I left twenty-five years before. People young and old were desiring the things of Jehovah God. It was common to see young people offering Christian leaflets at religious Hindu celebrations. During the day, they went to church and after service from 2:30 pm they returned at approximately 3:00 am. Hindu's and Muslims would also come to our services to get healing and find deliverance. People were open to hearing preaching from the Word of God and receiving teaching from the Holy Bible. I became aware of these Indian churches and communicated with their pastors by phone and through email. I networked with the United Pentecostal Churches in finding American preachers that were willing to go to India on behalf of the Indian Pastors to speak at their annual conferences. We were very successful, with God's help. I was glad that preachers in America had a burden for my country; giving their spiritual support to the Indian preachers. I met an Indian pastor of a very small and humble church. There was so much poverty and the needs of the people were so great that I made a personal commitment to send money. We are so blessed in America. Believe that "Nothing is impossible." If you want to give, do so cheerfully by faith and give it in secret. No one knew about my commitment for many years. Never expect to give for personal gain or to receive glory or praise from others. Give with a pure heart and do not bargain with God.

> *"Therefore when thou doest thine alms, do not sound a trumpet before*
> *thee, as the hypocrites do in the synagogues and in the streets, that they*
> *may have glory of men. Verily I say unto you, They have their reward.*
> *But when thou doest alms, let not thy left hand know what thy right*
> *hand doeth: That thine alms may be in secret: and thy Father which*
> *seeth in secret himself shall reward thee openly." (Matthew 6:2-4)*

God had allowed things to happen in my life, so that I could stay home. I look back with amazement of how my illnesses progressed where I could no longer walk, think, or feel normal until the day Brother James prayed and God lifted me out of a wheel chair. Still considered disabled with the tumors and blood disease, I lived on a meager monthly disability check. My check did not matter, since God took away my job, my worry was how I was going to pay my bills. Jesus spoke to me twice saying, "I will take care of you". Living in California or Texas, Jesus would supply all my needs. God did it out of His riches and abundance. I placed my trust in God for all of my day-to-day needs.

But seek ye first the kingdom of God, and his righteousness; and all these things shall be added unto you. (Mathew 6:33)

Before I left India, some of the ladies of the church told me that they were no longer buying luxuries for themselves. They were satisfied with whatever they had to wear because they received so much satisfaction from giving to the poor.

But godliness with contentment is great gain. For we brought nothing into this world, and it is certain we can carry nothing out. And having food and raiment let us be therewith content. (1 Tim.6:6-8)

The elderly and young children were also involved in projects of love. They got together to make gift packages to give to the poor. They were so content with the blessing of giving.

"Give, and it shall be given unto you; good measure, pressed down, and shaken together, and running over, shall men give into your bosom. For with the same measure that ye met withal it shall be measured to you again." (Luke 6:38)

Just imagine what occurred in such a relatively short time. I sold my home and purchased a new home in another state. I saw my country changed with people thirsty for the Lord Jesus Christ. Now I was anticipating starting a new life in Texas. When we put God first, the Lord of Glory will also be faithful to us.

Elizabeth Das

Back to America.

I returned from India three months later. I flew to Texas when my house was ready. On April 26, 2005, while my plane was landing at the Dallas-Ft. Worth Airport, I was crying because I was totally separated from all of my family and friends since first coming to this country. Then God gave me the following scripture:

But now thus saith the LORD that created thee, O Jacob, and he that formed thee, O Israel, Fear not: for I have redeemed thee, I have called thee by thy name; thou art mine. When thou passest through the waters, I will be with thee; and through the rivers, they shall not overflow thee: when thou walkest through the fire, thou shalt not be burned; neither shall the flame kindle upon thee. For I am the LORD thy God, the Holy One of Israel, thy Saviour: I gave Egypt for thy ransom, Ethiopia and Seba for thee. Since thou wast precious in my sight, thou hast been honourable, and I have loved thee: therefore will I give men for thee, and people for thy life. Fear not: for I am with thee: I will bring thy seed from the east, and gather thee from the west; I will say to the north, Give up; and to the south, Keep not back: bring my sons from far, and my daughters from the ends of the earth;
(Isaiah 43:1-6)

The day I arrived I found myself alone in that big new house. Reality sunk in as I stood in the middle of the living room and saw my house completely empty. I sat down on the floor and began to cry. I felt so alone and wanted to go back home to California where I had left my dear mother. We lived together for so long and she was a big part of me. I was so overwhelmed by this feeling of separation that I wanted to leave for the airport and fly back to California. I no longer wanted this house. My sorrow was bigger than my reality. While I was going through these feelings, God reminded me that I needed to call Brother Blakey. Brother Blakey did not know how I was feeling that exact moment but God did. I was surprised when he said, "Now Sister Das, you know that you are only a phone call away from us." His words were completely anointed because my pain and all of my despair disappeared instantly. I felt that I had a family, I was not alone, and that everything would be all right. From that day, the Blakey family accepted me into their own family at a time when I had no one.

My sister and her family later moved to Plano, Texas only a few miles from Wylie. The Blakey family consists of eleven brothers and sisters. Their children and grandchildren all treated me like family. They numbered close to 200 and everyone knows about the Blakey Family in Wylie. They have been a tremendous support to me and I have always been made to feel like a "Blakey" too! Once settled into my home, I had to find a church. I asked God which church He wanted for me. I visited many churches. Finally I visited a church in the city of Garland, The North Cities United Pentecostal Church. God clearly said, "This is your church." This is still where I congregate. I love my church and found a wonderful pastor, Rev. Hargrove. The Blakey Family became my extended family inviting me to lunch or to dinner after Church. They included me in their family reunions and family holidays too. God has wonderfully provided everything I need.

I thank God for my new Pastor, church, and the Blakey's who have adopted me into their family. I now live comfortably in my new home. God has kept His promise, "I will take care of you." God chose all this for me, according to His will for my life. Now I work for Him from the time I wake up at 3:50 a.m. to pray. I have breakfast and prepare to do the Lord's work from my office at home. My friends will tell you, "Never tell Sister Liz that she does not have a real job." What is my response? I work for the Lord, I put in long hours without punching a time clock, and I do not get a paycheck. God takes care of me and my reward will be in heaven.

I appreciate my job and love what I do!

Chapter 12

Demonic Deliverance And The Healing Power Of God

One Sunday afternoon I received a telephone call from Mr. Patel who was requesting that we go and pray for his father, who was attacked by demonic spirits. Mr. Patel is an engineer who has lived in America for over 30 years. He had heard of my healing and was open to hear about the Lord Jesus Christ. The following day, we went to his brother's house where we met with Mr. Patel and his family, (brother, the brother's wife, two sons and his father and mother). While everyone listened, another brother who was also a Christian began speaking about how he came to know Jesus. The father, the elder Mr. Patel, said he had worshiped idol gods but always felt bad when he performed the worship. He said he felt as though a rod was poking his stomach causing him pain and when he walked it felt as though he had rocks under his feet. We began to pray for him in the Name of the Lord Jesus Christ. We prayed until he was free from the demonic spirit and he began to feel much better. Before leaving, he received a Bible study so that he would understand the power of the Lord's name and how to stay free of demonic attacks from returning.

We were pleased when the son and one of the grandsons insisted that the elder Mr. Patel call out the name of JESUS but he would not; although he did not have any problem saying "God" (Bhagvan). The grandsons insisted, "No, say in the Name of Jesus" as the sons lined up to receive prayer. One of the grandsons who was in his twenty's had previously been in a car accident. He had been to many surgeons regarding a problem with his knee. That day, the Lord Jesus healed his knee and Mr. Patel's younger brother was greatly touched by God's Spirit. Everyone received prayer and testified how they were moved by God's Spirit working miracles of healing and deliverance that day. When the Lord Jesus walked among men, He taught and preached the gospel of the Kingdom to come and healed all manner of sickness and diseases among the people. He healed and delivered those who were possessed and tormented by demons and those that were lunatic (insane), and those that had the palsy, (Matthew 4:23-24). As disciples of God today, we continue to do His work and teach others about salvation in the name of our Lord Jesus.

*"Neither is there salvation in any other: for there is none other **name** under heaven given among men, whereby we must be saved."*
(Acts 4:12).

There are many benefits to serving the Living God. Instead of a god made of rock or stone that cannot see or cannot hear, we have the true and living God who searches the hearts of men and women. Open your heart and mind to listening to His voice. Pray that He will touch your heart. Pray that He will forgive you for rejecting Him. Pray to know Him and fall in love with Him. Do these now, for the doors will soon close.

Chapter 13

Confession And A Clean Conscience

One day an Indian couple came to visit and pray with me. As we got ready to pray, the wife began to pray out loud. The husband followed. I noticed that they both prayed in the same religious manner, but still I did enjoy listening to their eloquent words. I asked God, sincerely "I want you to pray through my mouth." When it was my turn to pray out loud the Holy Ghost took over and prayed in the Spirit.

"Likewise the Spirit also helpeth our infirmities: for we know not what we should pray for as we ought: but the Spirit itself maketh intercession for us with groaning which cannot be uttered. And he that searcheth the hearts knoweth what is the mind of the Spirit, because he maketh intercession for the saints according to the will of God."
(Romans 8:26, 27).

I was praying in the Spirit with the power of God in a way that exposed sin. The husband, who could no longer bare it, began confessing his sin to his wife, who was shocked. I later spoke with them about cleansing through his confession of sin.

"If we confess our sins, He is faithful and just to forgive us our sins and to cleanse us from all unrighteousness. If we say that we have not sinned, we make him a liar and his word is not in us." (1 John 1:9, 10)

I explained to the husband that, since he confessed, God would forgive him.

Also remember to confess your sins only to those who can pray over you.

Confess your faults one to another, and pray one for another, that ye may be healed. The effectual fervent prayer of a righteous man availeth much. (James 5:16)

I explained that once he was baptized, God would remove his sin and he would have a clean conscience.

"The like figure whereunto even baptism doth also now save us (not the putting away of the filth of the flesh, but the answer of a good conscience toward God) by the resurrection of Jesus Christ." (1 Peter 3:21)

A few days later, both husband and wife got baptized in the name of the Lord Jesus. The husband was totally delivered and his sins forgiven. They have both become such a blessing to the Kingdom of God.

"Repent and be baptized every one of you in the name of Jesus Christ for the remission of sins and ye shall receive the gift of the Holy Ghost." (Acts 2:38)

God is looking for those who will humble themselves before Him. It does not matter how eloquent and beautiful the words you pray are, but that you pray with your whole heart. He also knows what is in the heart when you pray. Remove sin by asking God for forgiveness, or your prayers will be hindered by the Holy Spirit. As believers, we search our hearts daily and judge ourselves. God is always there to forgive and cleanse us when we sin.

Chapter 14.

At The Edge Of Death

B rother James, whom I spoke of earlier, has the gift of healing through the anointing power of God. He was invited to pray for a Korean lady who was in the Queen of the Valley hospital Intensive Care Unit (ICU). According to the doctors, she was near death. Her funeral arrangements were already being made by her family. I accompanied Brother James that day and saw her body on life support; she was unconscious and close to the edge of death. When I began to pray, I felt as though something wanted to pick me up by my leg and throw me out of the room; but the power of the Holy Ghost was very strong in me and did not allow this spirit to have its way.

Ye are of God, little children, and have overcome them: because greater is he that is in you, than he that is in the world. (1 John 4:4)

After praying, the Lord spoke through me and I said these words, "This machinery will change." This was referring to the life support equipment that was attached to her body. I heard myself say these words as God has spoken the fate of this very ill woman. Brother James prayed for her and then we spoke to the lady's family about the power of prayer and the Word of God. They listened as I told them about my own healing and how God took me from a wheel chair to walking again. Their son who was an airline pilot was also present, but did not speak Korean. I spoke to him in English while the rest of the family conversed in Korean. Interestingly, he explained to me that his mother was supposed to travel to Canada the same day she became very ill. He explained that she had called out to her husband for help and was taken to the hospital although she refused to go. The son said his mother was telling them, "They will kill me at the hospital." She was certain that she would die if taken to the hospital. Her son continued to explain to us that she had told them, that every night; the people dressed in black were coming into the house. Every night his mother would yell out to both him and his father and angrily throw dishes at them for no apparent reason. She also began to write checks in a language that they could not understand. The behavior she exhibited was very bizarre. I explained to him about demonic spirits that can take over and torment a person. This astonished him, because as he explained to us, they all go to church and she gives so much money but they had never heard of this before. Demons are subject to true believers who have the Holy Ghost; because the Blood of Jesus is on their lives and they minister under the authority of the Name of Jesus in the power of His Name.

I told the young man that Brother James and I could pray in Jesus Name to cast out the demon and he agreed to the prayer of deliverance for his mother. When the doctor came to see his patient, he was amazed that she was responding and could not understand what had happened to his patient. The family told him that somebody had come to pray for her during the night and she started responding just like they were told that she would. A few days later, we had another opportunity to pray for the same lady. She was smiling as we came into the room. I then laid my hand on her head and started praying; she threw my hand away and moved her head up, pointing to the ceiling, because she couldn't speak. Her expression changed and she looked so terrified. After we left, her condition became worse. Her children were wondering what she was seeing and they asked her if she had seen something evil. She signals with her hand "yes". Again we returned to pray for her because she was terrified of her tormentor, a demonic spirit in her room. After praying this time, she was victoriously free from her tormentors. Thanks to the God that answers prayer. We later heard that she was released from the hospital, went into a rehabilitation program and was sent home where she continues to do well. She had pulled out of the edge of death.

Go testify unto the world:

*And he charged them that they should tell no man: but the more he charged them, so much the more a great deal they **published** it; (Mark 7:36)*

*Return to thine own house, and shew how great things God hath done unto thee. And he went his way, and **published** throughout the whole city how great things Jesus had done unto him. (Luke 8:39)*

The Bible says, we must go out and witness. This Korean family testified to other families about this miracle. One-day Bro. James received a call from another Korean lady. The husband of this family had a violent behavior and did not know what he was doing. His wife was a very petite and sweet lady. Some days he would try to kill her. Many times they had to take her to the hospital because he would beat her unmercifully. Since she heard about this miracle she invited us and asked for me. We went to see her and her husband. Bro. James asked me to speak and he prayed. We were all blessed. A few weeks later his wife called and asked if we would come again since her husband was doing better. So we went again and I gave my testimony about forgiveness and Bro. James prayed over all of them.

I shared with them about the time I was working and a woman supervisor; she harassed me unmercifully and I could not sleep at night. One day I went to my room to pray for her. Jesus said, "You need to forgive her". First it seemed hard and I thought, if I forgive her she will still keep doing the same thing to me. Since I heard Jesus talking to me I said, "Lord I forgive her completely" and God in His mercy helped me to forget it. As I forgave her I started sleeping well, not only that, but whenever she did wrong, it did not bother me.

The Bible says.

The thief cometh not, but for to steal, and to kill, and to destroy: I am come that they might have life, and that they might have it more abundantly (John 10:10)

I was happy that the mother in law was there to hear this testimony for her heart was heavy with sadness. It was so amazing to see the hand of God come in and change this whole situation and forgiveness swept over their hearts and love came inside them.

But if ye do not forgive, neither will your Father which is in heaven forgive your trespasses. (Mark 11:26)

Unforgiveness is a very dangerous thing. You will loose your soundness of mind and body. Forgiveness is for your benefit, not just for your enemy. God ask us to forgive so we can sleep better. To take revenge is His, not ours.

Judge not, and ye shall not be judged: condemn not, and ye shall not be condemned: forgive, and ye shall be forgiven: (Luke 6:37)

And the prayer of faith shall save the sick, and the Lord shall raise him up; and if he have committed sins, they shall be forgiven him. Confess your faults one to another, and pray one for another, that ye may be healed. The effectual fervent prayer of a righteous man availeth much. (James 5:15, 16)

In the latter part of the above story, we heard that her husband was completely healed from his mental problem and was so kind and loving to his wife.

Praise The Lord! Jesus brought peace in their home.

Chapter 15

Peace In God's Presence

T he presence of God can bring peace to the soul. I once prayed
for a gentleman who was terminally ill in the final stages of
cancer. He was the husband of a lady in the church. The lady
and her son at one time stayed with me in my home.

They had belonged to a church that did not believe in changing their lives
until they watched a video about the End Time. They both received the
revelation of Baptism in the name of the Lord Jesus, and began looking
for a church that would baptize them in Jesus' name. This is when they
found the church that I attend. Satan does not want anyone to have the
knowledge of the truth because it leads to salvation. He wants you to be
in darkness, thinking that you are saved while believing in false doctrines
and traditions of man. He will come against you when you are looking
for Truth. In this situation, the instrument used against this mother and
son was the unbelieving husband and father, who constantly harassed
and ridiculed them about their belief in God. Many times they would end
up coming to my home to pray and ended up staying. One day his son
heard the Lord saying to him, His days are numbered. The father was at
Baylor Hospital, in Dallas, Texas, Intensive Care Unit (ICU). He made
it very clear to them that he did not want prayer or any church people to

come around to pray. One day I asked the wife if I could visit and pray for her husband. She explained to me how he felt and said no. We continued to pray that God would soften his hardened heart.

One day I went to the hospital with the son and his wife and took a chance that God had changed him. The son asked his father, *Dad do you want Sister Elizabeth to pray for you? She is a prayer warrior.* Since his father could no longer speak, he asked his father to wink his eyes so that he could communicate with him. He then asked him to wink to signal to us if he wanted me to pray for him, he winked. I began to pray asking that his sins be washed in the Blood of Jesus. I noticed some change in him and continued to pray until the presence of the Holy Ghost was in the room. After I prayed, the father was trying to communicate by pointing to the ceiling as if showing us something. He tried to write but couldn't. The son asked his father to wink if it was something that was good that he was seeing. He winked! Then he asked his father to wink if it is light, but he did not wink. Then he asked him if it were angels that he was seeing and to wink. But he did not wink. Finally the son asks if it is the Lord Jesus. His father then winked his eyes.

The following week I went to the hospital to see him again. This time, he was very different and had a peaceful countenance about him. A few days later he died in peace. God in his mercy and love gave him peace before his passing away. We do not know what goes on between someone so very ill and his Maker. The presence of the Lord was in that room. I saw a man that was hardened against God and his own family, but at death's door, the Lord made Himself known to him, giving him the knowledge of His existence.

O give thanks unto the LORD; for he is good: for his mercy endureth forever. O give thanks unto the God of gods: for his mercy endureth forever. O give thanks to the Lord of lords: for his mercy endureth forever. To him who alone doeth great wonders: for his mercy endureth forever. (Psalm 136:1-4)

Chapter 16.

A Sacrificial Life Style in Living

D uring this time, I was doing a Bible study on hair, clothing, jewelry and makeup. I said to myself, "These people are old fashioned." I knew in my heart that I loved God; therefore, what I wear should not matter. Time passed and one day I heard the (Rhyma) Spirit of God speak to my heart "you do what you feel in your heart." At that moment my eyes were opened. I understood I had a love for the world in my heart and I was conforming myself to the world's fashions. (Rhyma is the illuminated and anointed Word of God that has been spoken to you for a specific time or situation.)

O LORD, thou hast searched me, and known me. Thou knowest my downsitting and mine uprising, thou understandest my thought afar off. Thou compassest my path and my lying down, and art acquainted with all my ways. (Psalm 139:1-3)

Jewelry:

I did not like jewelry, so it was not hard getting rid of the few pieces that I had.

*Likewise, ye wives, be in subjection to your own husbands; that, if any obey not the word, they also may without the word be won by the conversation of the wives; While they behold your chaste conversation coupled with fear. Whose adorning let it not be that **outward** adorning of plaiting the hair, and of wearing of gold, or of putting on of apparel; But let it be the hidden man of the heart, in that which is not corruptible, even the **ornament** of a meek and quiet spirit, which is in the sight of God of great price. For after this manner in the old time the holy women also, who trusted in God, adorned themselves, being in subjection unto their own husbands: Even as Sara obeyed Abraham, calling him lord: whose daughters ye are, as long as ye do well, and are not afraid with any amazement. (1 Peter 3:1-6)*

In like manner also, that women adorn themselves in modest apparel, with shamefacedness and sobriety; not with broided hair, or gold, or pearls, or costly; array; But (which becometh women professing godliness) with good works. (1Timothy 2:9, 10)

Hair

*Doth not even nature itself teach you, that, if a man have long hair, it is a shame unto him? But if a woman have long hair, it is a glory to her: for her hair is given her for a **covering**. (1 Corinthians 11:14, 15)*

In my younger years I always had long hair. At the age of twenty, I got my first haircut and continued cutting my hair until it was very short. So the teaching on uncut hair was hard for me to accept at first. I did not want to let my hair grow because I liked short hair. It was easy to take care of. I started asking God to please let me wear short hair. But to my surprise, God changed my way of thinking by putting His Word in my heart and it was no longer hard for me to let my hair grow.

During this time my mother was living with me. Since I did not know how to take care of my long hair my mom would ask me to cut it because she did not like the way it looked. I started studying more about hair from the Bible. I received a better understanding and knowledge, which helped my convictions grow stronger in my heart.

I prayed and ask the Lord, *"What should I do about my mom since she does not like my long hair"*? He spoke to me and said, *"Pray that her thinking would change."*

> *Trust in the LORD with all thine heart; and lean not unto thine own understanding. In all thy ways acknowledge him, and he shall direct thy paths. (Proverb 3:5, 6)*

The Lord is my counselor so I continued to pray that her thinking would change.

Jesus is our Counselor;

> *For unto us a child is born, unto us a son is given: and the government shall be upon his shoulder: and his name shall be called Wonderful, **Counseller**, The mighty God, The everlasting Father, The Prince of Peace. (Isaiah 9:6)*

I did not cut my hair anymore. My hair continued grow and one day my mom said to me, "you look nice with long hair!" I was very happy to hear those words. I knew the Lord had directed me in prayer and had answered my prayer. I know my uncut hair is my glory and I have been given power on my head because of the Angels.

I know when I pray there is power. Praise The Lord!!!

*But every woman that prayeth or prophesieth with her head **uncovered** dishonoureth her head: for that is even all one as if she were shaven. But if a woman have long hair, it is a glory to her: **for her hair is given her for a covering**. (1st Corinthians 11:5,15,)*

This scripture is very clear that uncut hair is our covering and not a scarf, hat or veil. It represents our submission to the authority of God and His glory. Throughout God's Word you will find that angels protected the Glory of God. Wherever the glory of God was, Angels were present. Our uncut hair is our glory and Angels are always present to protect us because of our submission to the Word of God. These Angels are protecting us and our family.

For this cause ought the woman to have power on her head because of the angels. (1st Corinthians 11:10)

1st Corinthians 11 is God's orderly thought and action for maintaining an unambiguous distinction between female and male.

The New Testament shows that women had uncut long hair.

*And, behold, a woman in the city, which was a sinner when she knew that Jesus sat at meat in the Pharisee's house, brought an alabaster box of ointment, And stood at his feet behind him weeping, and began to wash his feet with tears, and did **wipe them with the hairs of her head**, and kissed his feet, and anointed them with the ointment. (Luke 7:37, 38)*
he Lords Says

"Cut off thine hair, O Jerusalem, and cast it away, and take up a lamentation on high places; for the LORD hath rejected and forsaken the generation of his wrath." (Jeremiah 7; 29)

Cut hair is a symbol of shame, disgrace, and mourning. Cutting the hair represents an ungodly and shameful act of backslidden people of God. It is a sign that the Lord has rejected them. Remember we are His bride.

Encyclopedia Britannica, V, 1033 states, after WW I "hair was bobbed". The Cutting of hair was adopted by almost all women everywhere.

God's Words are established for eternity. God's requirements for women is to have uncut long hair and men to have short hair.

Clothing

God's Word instructs us on how we dress as well. When I was a new convert and learning how we should dress I was not convicted about my clothes. Because of my type of work I would wear pants. I thought to myself "*It would be okay if I continued to wear pants to work only.*" I bought some new pants and received many compliments on how nice I looked. I already knew women should not wear men's apparel. Pants have always been men's clothing, not women's. Once you have the word of God planted in your heart you will receive a conviction on proper apparel to wear.

The woman shall not wear that which pertaineth unto a man, neither shall a man put on a woman's garment: for all that do so [are] ***abomination*** *unto the LORD thy God. (Deuteronomy 22:5)*

Confusion started when men and women started wearing unisex clothing. The next step will lead you, as God said, to:

Leviticus 18:22 Thou shalt not lie with mankind, as with womankind: it is ***abomination.***

We will be affected by what we wear. The word abomination is used to describe the woman who wears "that which pertaineth unto a man" and the man who puts on "a woman's garment." God knows each step of sexual confusion. God has made both genders completely different with a different purpose. Did you notice that it was women who started putting on pants first? This is just like when Eve was disobedient in the Garden of Eden! This confusion is a proof of today's society we are living in. Sometimes you cannot tell the difference between men and women.

Over 70 years ago, women's clothing was not an issue, because they basically wore long dresses or long skirts. No confusion. As women started wearing men's clothing, they started acting like men and men as women. This is disorder.

They shall have linen bonnet upon their heads, and shall have linen **breeches** *upon their loins; they shall not gird themselves with anything that causeth sweat (Ezekiel 44:18)*

Today's perverse disobedient media driven generation is learning from the prince of the air, which is Satan. They are not aware of the truth in the Bible. Also their supporters are false teachers teaching the doctrine and commandment of man and not of God.

Behold, thou hast made my days as an handbreadth; and mine age is as nothing before thee: verily every man at his best state is altogether vanity. Selah. Surely every man walketh in a vain shew: surely they are disquieted in vain: he heapeth up riches, and knoweth not who shall gather them. (Psalms 39:5-6)

When Adam and Eve disobeyed The Lord, and ate the fruit of the forbidden tree they knew that they had sinned and their eyes were opened to their nakedness.

And the eyes of them both were opened, and they knew that they were naked; and they sewed fig leaves together, and made themselves aprons (Genesis 3: 7).

Adam and Eve covered themselves with fig leaves. They made aprons of fig leaves, which was insufficient. God has a standard of covering and therefore He did not approve of their improper covering of fig leaves.....
So He clothed them with coats of skin.

Unto Adam also and to his wife did the LORD God make coats of skins, and clothed them. (Genesis 3: 21)

The enemy of our soul, the Devil, enjoys causing immodest exposure of the body.

*Luke 8:35 "Then they went out to see what was done; and came to Jesus, and found the man, out of whom the devils were departed, sitting at the feet of Jesus, **clothed**, and in his right mind: and they were afraid."*

When a person does not cover their body it proves that they are influenced by the wrong spirit which produces wrong motives.

It is very important that we should always read the Word of God, pray without ceasing, and fast for a better understanding and leading of His spirit. Transformation comes through the word of God, which first comes from the inside, and then change comes to the outside.

This book of the law shall not depart out of thy mouth; but thou shalt meditate therein day and night, that thou mayest observe to do according to all that is written therein: for then thou shalt make thy way prosperous, and then thou shalt have good success. (Joshua 1:8)

Satan's attack is on the Word of God. Remember Eve? The devil knows what to attack and when to attack because he is subtle and cunning.

Be sober, be vigilant; because your adversary the devil, as a roaring lion, walketh about, seeking whom he may devour: (1 Peter 5:8)

He that hath my commandments, and keepeth them, he it is that loveth me: and he that loveth me shall be loved of my Father, and I will love him, and will manifest myself to him. (John 14:21)

If ye keep my commandments, ye shall abide in my love; even as I have kept my Father's commandments, and abide in his love. (John 15:10)

That evening while I was at work, a thought came to my mind. I wondered how I looked in the eyes of God. All of a sudden shame came upon me and I could not look up. I felt as if I was standing before The Lord our God. As you know we hear through our ears, but I heard His voice, as though He were speaking through every cell of my body saying,

"I love you sincerely". When I heard these beautiful words from God saying "I love you sincerely", it meant so much to me. I could hardly wait to get out of work and go home so I could completely clean out my closet of all my worldly clothes.

For a couple of weeks I kept hearing the echo of His voice telling me, "I love you sincerely." Later it faded away.

Living for God is not just what we speak, but it is a life style. When God spoke to Moses, He spoke very clearly to him. Moses knew without a doubt, the voice of God.

The word shamefacedness translated from Greek refers to a sense of shame or modesty, or the inner decency recognizing that the lack of clothing is shameful. This means our outer appearance reflects our inward being not only to ourselves but also to others. This is why the Bible says that modest clothing is similar with shamefacedness

Proverb 7:10 And, behold, there met him a woman with the attire of an harlot, and subtil of heart.

*In like manner also, that women adorn themselves in modest apparel, with **shamefacedness** and **sobriety**; not with broided hair, or gold, or pearls, or costly array; (1 Timothy 2:9)*

Clothing must cover a person's nakedness. Sobriety would keep one from wearing that which is intended to look sexy or is a revealing fashion. Today's style of clothing is cut so short that it will remind you of the clothing of a prostitute. It is all about how sexy one looks. Clothing designers are making the style of clothing more revealing and more provocative.

Thank God for His word which He has established for eternity; He knows the generations of all ages. The Word will keep you from conforming to this world.

Elizabeth Das

The definition of modesty changes between country, time, and generation. Asian women wear loose pants and long blouses called Panjabi dresses, which are very modest. Arab ladies wear long robes with a veil. Western Christian ladies wear their dresses below their knees.

We still have God fearing Christian ladies who love to be modest and keep the preaching and teaching of God.

Prove all things; hold fast that which is good. (1 Thessalonians 5:21)

We are living in a shocking time where there is no fear of God.

If ye love me, keep my commandments. (John 14:15)

Paul said,

*"For ye are bought with a price: therefore, glorify God in your **body**, and in your spirit, which are God's." (1 Corinthians 6: 20)*

Clothing should not be tight, short nor low cut. Images on some shirts and blouses are often improperly placed.

God's ideas of making us wear clothing are to be covered up. Remember Eve and Adam were naked. We are not innocent any more. We know this is the temptation to the eye of the man. David saw Bathsheba without clothes and he fell into adultery.

The fashion of clothing for young women or little girls of our time is immodest. The pants are tightly worn. The Bible says teach children the righteousness of God. Instead of teaching girls modesty, parents shop for immodest clothes.

The Godly conscientious Christian woman will choose her clothing that is pleasing to Christ and her husband. She no longer desires to wear what is "in fashion".

92

Immodest clothing, jewelry, and make up feed the lust of the eyes, lust of the flesh, and the pride of life.

*Love not the world, neither the things that are in the world. If any man love the world, the love of the Father is not in him. **For all that is in the world**, the **lust of the flesh**, and the **lust of the eyes**, and the **pride of life**, is not of the Father, but is of the world. And the world passeth away, and the lust thereof: but he that doeth the will of God abideth forever. (1 John 2:15-17)*

Satan knows that man is visually oriented. Women do not see the intention of Satan. Immodesty is a powerful temptation and enticement to men. Immodest clothing, jewelry, and makeup cause excitement for men. Pride and vanity builds up the human ego. A woman feels powerful because she can attract the lustful attention of men. These things make a woman proud of her outward appearance.

I beseech you therefore, brethren, by the mercies of God, that ye present your bodies a living sacrifice, holy, acceptable unto God, which is your reasonable service. And be not conformed to this world: but be ye transformed by the renewing of your mind, that ye may prove what is that good, and acceptable, and perfect, will of God. (Romans 12:1, 2)

Make up

The Bible definitely talks **against** make up. In the Bible, make up is always associated with ungodly women. In the Bible, Jezebel was a wicked woman who painted her face.

Through His Word, God has given us Christians, written instructions regarding the painting of the face which is now called makeup. God has informed us of every detail with even historical references. The Bible considers us as a light of this world; if we are that light we do not need painting. Nobody paints the light bulb. A dead thing needs painting. You can paint the wall, wood, etc.

Most women and little girls wear makeup these days, without any knowledge of history or the Bible. Make up was used only on the face; but now, they like to paint and print different parts of the body such as the arms, hands, feet, etc. Is make up sinful? God cares what you do to your body. God clearly states His opposition on painting and piercing of the body, and applying makeup, and tattoos.

*Ye shall not make any cuttings in your flesh for the dead, **nor print any marks upon you**: I am the LORD. (Leviticus 19:28).*

I never wore makeup, but I did wear lipstick because I liked it. When I heard preaching about make up, I began to wear less lipstick and later completely stopped. In my heart, I still had the desire to wear it, but I did not.

In prayer, I asked God How He felt about lipstick. One day two ladies were walking towards me and I noticed them wearing lipstick. At that moment, I saw through His spiritual eyes, how it looked…. I felt so sick to my stomach. I was highly convicted in my heart and I never again had the desire to wear lipstick. My desire was to please Him and to obey His Word.

"So speak ye, and so do, as they that shall be judged by the law of liberty" (James 2:12)

Even though we have the liberty to do as we choose and live as we would like; our heart is deceitful and our flesh will seek after the things of this world. We know our flesh is enmity against God and the things of God. We must always walk in the spirit in order not to fulfill the lust of the flesh. The devil is not the problem. We are our own problem, if we walk in the flesh.

For all that is in the world, the lust of the flesh, and the lust of the eyes, and the pride of life, is not of the Father, but is of the world. And the world passeth away, and the lust thereof: but he that doeth the will of God abideth forever. (1stJohn 2:16-17)

Satan wants to be the center of everything. He was perfect in beauty and full of pride. He knows what caused him to fall and he also uses that to make you fall.

*Son of man, take up a lamentation upon the king of Tyrus, and say unto him, Thus saith the Lord GOD; Thou sealest up the sum, full of wisdom, and **perfect in beauty**. Thou hast been in Eden the garden of God; every precious stone was thy covering, the sardius, topaz, and the diamond, the beryl, the onyx, and the jasper, the sapphire, the emerald, and the carbuncle, and gold: the workmanship of thy tabrets and of thy pipes was prepared in thee in the day that thou wast created (Ezekiel 28:12,13)*

When we walk in the flesh we seek to be the center of attention as well. This can be seen in our clothing, conversation, and actions. We easily fall into Satan's trap by conforming to the world and its worldly fashions.

Let me share how and where make up or painting started. Wearing makeup started in Egypt. Kings and queens wore make up around their eyes. Egyptian eye makeup was used for protection from evil magic, and also as a symbol of the new birth in reincarnation. It was also used by those that dressed the dead. They wanted the dead to appear as though they were just sleeping.

You need to know what the Bible clearly states about this subject. If makeup is important to God, it has to be mentioned in His Word—both specifically and in principle.

And when Jehu was come to Jezreel, Jezebel heard of it; and she painted her face, and tired her head, and looked out at a window. (2 Kings 9:30)

The young man, Jehu then went straight away to Jezreel to execute judgment over Jezebel. When she heard that she was in danger, she put on makeup; but her makeup failed to seduce Jehu. What the prophet of God prophesied over Jezebel and her husband King Ahab came to pass.

Her abomination came to an end as the prophet of God prophesied over them. When Jehu had her thrown from a window, the dogs ate her flesh; as God had declared! Make up is a self destructive weapon.

Lust not after her beauty in thine heart; neither let her take thee with her eyelids. (Proverbs 6:25)

"And when thou art spoiled, what wilt thou do? Though thou clothest thyself with crimson, though thou deckest thee with ornaments of gold, though thou rentest thy face with painting, in vain shalt thou make thyself fair; thy lovers will despise thee, they will seek thy life."
(Jeremiah 4:30)

History tells us that prostitutes painted their faces so they could be recognized as prostitutes. Over time, make up and face painting have become commonly used. It is no longer seen as improper.

And furthermore, that ye have sent for men to come from far, unto whom a messenger was sent; and, lo, they came: for whom thou didst wash thyself, paintedst thy eyes, and deckedst thyself with ornaments. (Ezekiel 23:40)

Makeup is "products nobody needs" but wanting them is human nature. Pride and vanity are why many women use makeup, so they can fit into the world. This is human nature. We all want to fit in!

Hollywood stars are responsible for such drastic changes in women's thinking of outer appearance. Make up was worn by only arrogant and conceited proud women. Everyone wants to look pretty, even children who wear makeup.

Pride and vanity has promoted the makeup industry, by welcoming makeup they have become vain. Anywhere you go you will find makeup. From the poorest to the richest, all want to look beautiful. Today's society puts too much emphasis on the outward appearance; because of inner insecurities, all ages of women apply makeup.

Many are depressed about their looks; they even attempt to commit suicide. Beauty is one of the most admired things for this generation. Some people wear makeup the minute they wake up. They do not like their natural look. Make up has possessed them so badly that without it they feel unwanted. This causes depression in our younger generation and even little children.

Now think of the most well-known righteous women of the Old or New Testament Bible. You will not find a single one who wore makeup. There is no mention of Sarah, Ruth, Abigail, Naomi, Mary, Deborah, Esther, Rebecca, Feebie or any other virtuous and meek woman ever applying makeup.

He will beautify the meek with Salvation (Psalms 149:4b)

In fact, in God's Word the only examples of those who wore makeup were adulteresses, harlots, those rebelling, backsliders and false prophetesses. This should serve as a great warning to anyone who cares about the Word of God and wishes to follow a Biblical righteous example instead of choosing to follow the example of ungodly women.

__Put on__ therefore, as the elect of God, holy and beloved, bowels of mercies, kindness, humbleness of mind, meekness, longsuffering; (Colossians 3:12)

Nay but, O man, who art thou that repliest against God? Shall the thing formed say to him that formed it, Why hast thou made me thus? (Romans 9:20)

Our body is the temple of God; we should desire to seek after the righteous ways of God. This is done by women presenting themselves in Holiness of dress, with open face (clean face), and reflecting Gods Precious Glory in our bodies.

> *What? know ye not that your body is the temple of the Holy Ghost*
> *which is in you, which ye have of God, and ye are not your*
> *own? (1 Corinthians 6:19)*

You and I are bought with a price and also God has created us in His image. The laws of God are to protect us and should be written in our hearts. You and I have rules and guidelines to live by, just as we who are parents have rules and guidelines for our children. When we choose to obey the laws and guidelines of God, we will be blessed and not punished.

> *"I call heaven and earth to record this day against you, that I have*
> *set before you life and death, blessing and cursing: therefore choose*
> *life, that both thou and thy seed may live" (Deuteronomy 30:19)*

Pride and rebellion will bring affliction of sickness, finance, oppression, and demonic possession upon us. When we seek after the things of this world through pride and rebellion, we are setting ourselves up for failure. It is the devils desire to corrupt our lives with the sin of pride. This is not Gods will for our life!

I have seen the changes when worldly women become Godly women. They become transformed from looking aged, depressed, stressed, tormented, and unhappy to looking more youthful, beautiful, vibrant, peaceful, and radiant women.

We have one life to live! Therefore, let's represent the God of Abraham, Jacob and Isaac…. presenting our bodies, a living sacrifice, Holy and acceptable in His sight. This is our reasonable service inwardly and outwardly, blameless in all things!

When we disobey Gods' Word through pride and rebellion, we bring curses upon ourselves, our children, and our children's children. This can be seen in Eve's disobedient and rebellious actions; the result was the flood that came upon the earth and all was destroyed. Samson and Saul brought destruction on themselves and their family by their disobedience. Eli's disobedience brought death to his sons and removal from the priesthood.

History through the Word of God tells us that before destruction, the mentality of the human race was haughty, selfcentered, and they were seeking their own pleasure.

*Moreover, the LORD saith, Because the **daughters of Zion** are haughty, and walk with stretched forth necks and wanton eyes, walking and mincing as they go, and making a tinkling with their feet: Therefore, the LORD will smite with a scab the crown of the head of the daughters of Zion, and the LORD will discover their secret parts. In that day the Lord will take away the bravery of their tinkling ornaments about their feet, and their cauls, and their round tires like the moon, The chains, and the bracelets, and the mufflers, The bonnets, and the ornaments of the legs, and the headbands, and the tablets, and the earrings, The rings, and nose jewels, The changeable suits of apparel, and the mantles, and the wimples, and the crisping pins, The glasses, and the fine linen, and the hoods, and the vails. And it shall come to pass, that instead of sweet smell there shall be stink; and instead of a girdle a rent; and instead of well set hair baldness; and instead of a stomacher a girding of sackcloth; and burning instead of beauty. Thy men shall fall by the sword, and thy mighty in the war. And her gates shall lament and mourn; and she being desolate shall sit upon the ground. (Isaiah 3:16-26)*

Our choices in life are very important. Making choices that are Bible based and Spirit led will bring blessing upon us and our children. Choose to rebel against the Word of God and seek your own selfish pleasure, then you will be repeating the History of:

1. Disobedient Eve who brought the Flood.

And God saw that the wickedness of man was great in the earth, and that every imagination of the thoughts of his heart was only evil continually. And it repented the LORD that he had made man on the earth, and it grieved him at his heart. And the LORD said, I will destroy man whom I have created from the face of the earth; both man, and beast, and the creeping thing, and the fowls of the air; for it repenteth me that I have made them. (Genesis 6:5-7)

2. The rebellion of Sodom and Gomorrah:

*Then the LORD rained upon **Sodom** and upon Gomorrah brimstone and fire from the LORD out of heaven; (Genesis 19:24)*

These are a few examples from the Bible. You know that you make a difference in this world. You do not want to revive evil ancient history.

This is what God has to about   rebellious and disobedience:

And I will send the sword, the famine, and the pestilence, among them, till they be consumed from off the land that I gave unto them and to their fathers (Jeremiah 24:10)

But to the Obedient:

And thou shalt return and obey the voice of the LORD, and do all his commandments which I command thee this day. And the LORD thy God will make thee plenteous in every work of thine hand, in the fruit of thy body, and in the fruit of thy cattle, and in the fruit of thy land, for good: for the LORD will again rejoice over thee for good, as he rejoiced over thy fathers: If thou shalt hearken unto the voice of the LORD thy God, to keep his commandments and his statutes which are written in this book of the law, and if thou turn unto the LORD thy God with all thine heart, and with all thy soul. For this commandment which I command thee this day, it is not hidden from thee, neither is it far off. (Deuteronomy 30:8-11)

Chapter 17

Travel Ministry: Called To Teach And Spread The Gospel

I am not a minister in the sense of one who is called a reverend, pastor, or preacher. When we receive the Holy Ghost and fire, we become ministers of His Word in spreading the Good News. Wherever I go, I ask God for the opportunity to be a witness and teacher of His Word. I always use the KJV Bible since it is the only source that quickens the heart and mind of the human. When the seeds are planted, it is impossible for Satan to remove it, if we continuously water it with prayer.

When individuals accept this marvelous truth, I get them connected to a local church so they will be baptized in the ***Name of Jesus***; they can be under the discipleship of a Pastor to stay in contact with them. It is important to have a Pastor who will feed (teach) the Word of God and watch over them.

*"Go ye therefore and teach all nations, baptizing them in the **name** of the Father and of the Son and of the Holy Ghost." (Matthew 28:19)*

"And I will give you pastors according to mine heart, which shall feed you with knowledge and understanding." (Jeremiah 3:15)

When the Lord gives us instructions to do His will, it can be anywhere and at any time. His ways may not make any sense at times, but I have learned from experience, that this does not matter to me. From the time I wake up, to the time I walk out of my house, I never know what God has prepared for me. As Believers, we must grow in our faith through studying the Word, so that we may become mature teachers. We continue to reach higher levels of maturity by never missing an opportunity to witness to others; especially when God has opened the door.

"For when for the time ye ought to be teachers, ye have need that one teaches you again which be the first principles of the oracles of God; and are become such as have need of milk and not of strong meat. For every one that useth milk is unskillful in the word of righteousness: for he is a babe. But strong meat belongeth to them that are full age, even those who by reason of use have their senses exercised to discern both good and evil." (Hebrews 5:12-14)

In this chapter I am sharing with you a few of my traveling experiences with a few important historical points that have been interjected to explain early church and subsequent doctrine beliefs.

God brought me back to visit California, by way of an "illogical flight plan". Due to health issues, I always prefer direct flights. This time I purchased a flight from Dallas - Ft. Worth, Texas to Ontario, California with a stopover in Denver, Colorado. I cannot explain why I did this, but later on it made sense. While on the plane, I made the stewardess aware that I was in pain and was seated near a rest room. During the latter part of the flight, I asked the stewardess if she could find a place for me to lie down. She led me to the back of the plane. The pain later subsided. The stewardess returned to see how I was feeling and told me that she had been praying for me.

The Lord was opening the door for me to share what He had done for me. I told her about my injuries, illnesses, and healings. She was so amazed that I had endured all of this without medication and only trusting in God. As we spoke about the Bible, she told me that she had never heard that anyone could receive the Holy Ghost. I explained that according to the Scriptures, it is for us even today. I told her my reason for leaving my home in India; when we seek God with all of our heart, He will answer our prayers. She was very nice and caring to me just like many other times when I have flown, there always seems to be someone on the flight that has shown me such kindness and care. I continued to tell her about the Holy Ghost and the evidence of speaking in tongues. She adamantly said shedid not believe it. I spoke to her about baptism in the Name of the Lord Jesus and she admitted that she had never heard of this either. The baptism of the apostles as spoken in Acts Chapter 2 is not preached by the majority of churches as most have adopted the Trinity doctrine of three persons in the Godhead and invoking the titles: Father, Son and Holy Spirit, when baptizing.

*"And Jesus came and spake unto them, saying, all power is given unto me in heaven and in earth. Go ye therefore, and teach all nations, baptizing them in the **name** of the Father, and of the Son, and of the Holy Ghost" (Matthew 28:18-19)*

When the disciples baptized in the Name of Jesus, they were fulfilling the baptism of the Father and of the Son and of the Holy Spirit when the person went into the water in full submersion. This was not some confusion; they were fulfilling what Jesus commanded them to do as the scriptures show.

*For there are three that bear record in heaven, the Father, the Word, and the Holy Ghost: and these **three are one**. (1 John 5:7)*

(This scripture has been removed from NIV and all modern translation of the Bible)

*"Now when they heard this, they were pricked in their heart, and said unto Peter and to the rest of the apostles, Men and brethren, what shall we do? Then Peter said unto them, Repent, and be baptized every one of you in **the name of Jesus Christ** for the remission of sins, and ye shall receive the gift of the Holy Ghost." (Acts 2:37-38)*

*"When they heard this, they were **baptized in the name of the Lord Jesus**. And when Paul had laid his hands upon them, the Holy Ghost came on them; and they spake with tongues, and prophesied. And all the men were about twelve." (Acts 19:5-7)*

*"For they heard them speak with tongues, and magnify God. Then answered Peter, can any man forbid water, that these should not be baptized, which have received the Holy Ghost as well as we? And he commanded them to be **baptized in the name of the Lord**. Then prayed they him to tarry certain days". (Acts 10:46-48)*

The apostles did not disobey Jesus. The Day of Pentecost was the beginning of the Church Age after Jesus had risen from the dead and was received unto glory. He had appeared to the Apostles and reprimanded them for their unbelief and was with them forty days. During that time, Jesus taught them many things. The Bible says, that believers should be baptized.

"Afterward he appeared unto the eleven as they sat at meat, and upbraided them with their unbelief and hardness of heart, because they believed not them which had seen him after he was risen. And he said unto them, Goye into all the world, and preach the gospel to every creature. He that believeth and is baptized shall be saved; but he that believeth not shall be damned." (Mark 16:14-16)

Man later adopted different baptismal formula including "sprinkling," instead of full submersion. (Some argument is because the Bible doesn't say you can't sprinkle and the Roman church baptized infants). Baptism in the name of Jesus was changed by the Roman Church when they adopted the trinity view.

Before I continue, first I wish to say that I do not question the sincerity of many wonderful Believers who seek a personal walk with our Lord, who love God and believe what they believe to be early biblical teaching. This is why it is so important to read and study the scriptures yourself, including the history of the Early Apostolic Church doctrine of the Bible. "Church Doctrine Goes into Apostasy."

Apostasy means to fall away from the truth. An apostate is someone who once believed and then rejected the truth of God.

In 312 AD when Constantine was the emperor, Christianity was adopted by Rome as the favored religion. Constantine cancelled the persecution decrees of Diocletian (Latin: Gaius Aurelius Valerius Diocletianus Augustus ;) that began in 303 AD. Diocletian was a Roman Emperor from 284-305 AD. The persecution decrees took away the rights of Christians and demanded them to follow "traditional religious practices," which included sacrificing to the Roman gods. This was the last official persecution of Christianity along with the killings and terrifying of those that would not comply. Constantine "Christianized" the Roman Empire and made it the religion of the state i.e. official religion. Under his rule he encouraged pagan religions as well in Rome. This strengthened Constantine's plan to have unification and peace in his empire. Thus, "Christianized Rome" and a political church were made to rule. With all this, Satan had designed a most powerful plan of corrupting the church from within with the early church not being recognized anywhere. Christianity was degraded, contaminated and weaken with a pagan system joining the world political system of that time. According to this system, baptism made anyone a Christian and they brought in their pagan religion, saints, and images in to the church. At a later stage, the Trinity Doctrine was also established in their council. The apostate church no longer recognized, preached, or gave any thought to the importance of the Holy Ghost or speaking in tongues. In 451 AD, at the Council of Chalcedon, with the approval of the Pope, the Nicene/Constantinople Creed was set as authoritative. No one was allowed to debate on the matter. To speak against the Trinity was now considered blasphemy.

Hard sentences ranging from mutilation to death were announced to those that disobeyed. Differences of belief arose between the Christians and this resulted in maiming and slaughtering of thousands. True believers had no other choice but to go underground in hiding from their persecutors who slaughtered in the name of Christianity.

I told her that the belief of trinity came from the Gentiles who were unaware about the ordinances, laws and commandments of God and was established in 325 AD when the First Council of Nicaea established the doctrine of the trinity as orthodoxy and adopted the Nicean Creed of the Roman Church.

The Trinity was put together after 300 bishops gathered and came up with it after six weeks.

No one can ever change a commandment! The early church in the Book of Acts began upon the Old Testament belief of the absolute Oneness of God along with the New Testament revelation of Jesus Christ, as being the one God Incarnate. The New Testament was completed and the last of the apostles had died toward the end of the first century. By the beginning of the fourth century, the primary doctrine of God in Christendom had gone from the biblical Oneness of God to an apparent belief of trinitarianism.

I marvel that ye are so soon removed from him that called you into the grace of Christ unto another gospel: Which is not another; but there be some that trouble you, and would pervert the gospel of Christ. But though we, or an angel from heaven, preach any other gospel unto you than that which we have preached unto you, let him be accursed. As we said before, so say I now again, if any man preach any other gospel unto you than that ye have received, let him be accursed.
(Galatians 1:6-9)

The writers of the Post-Apostolic Age (90-140 AD) were loyal to the biblical language, how it was used and thought of. They believed in

Monotheism, which is the absolute deity of Jesus Christ, and the manifestation of God in the Flesh.

Hear, O Israel: <u>The LORD our God is one LORD</u>: (Deuteronomy 6:4)

*And without controversy great is the mystery of godliness: **<u>God was manifest in the flesh</u>**, justified in the Spirit, seen of angels, preached unto the Gentiles, believed on in the world, received up into glory.*
(1 Timothy 3:16)

They connected great importance to the name of God and believed in baptism in the name of Jesus. The Early church converts were Jewish; they knew that Jesus was the "Lamb of God". God put on flesh so He could shed blood.

*"Take heed therefore unto yourselves, and to all the flock, over the which the Holy Ghost hath made you overseers, **to feed the church of God**, which he hath purchased with his **own blood** (Acts 20:28)*

The name Jesus means: Hebrew Yeshua, a Greek Yesous, an English Jesus. That is why Jesus said.

Jesus saith unto him, Have I been so long time with you, and yet hast thou not known me, Philip? he that hath seen me hath seen the Father; and how sayest thou then, Show us the Father? (John 14:9)

They did not support any idea of a trinity, or Trinitarian language as later adopted by the Church of Rome. Although the majority of Christian churches today follow the doctrine of the trinity, the early church still prevails of the apostolic doctrine of the Day of Pentecost. God warned us not to turn away from the faith. There is One God, One Faith and One Baptism.

*"One Lord, one faith, **one baptism**, One God and Father of all, who is above all, and through all, and in you all." (Ephesians 4:5-6)*

Elizabeth Das

> *"And Jesus answered him, the first of all the commandments is, Hear, O Israel; **The Lord our God is one Lord**:" (Mark 12:29)*

> *"Yet I am the LORD thy God from the land of Egypt, and thou shalt know no god but me: for there is **no saviour beside me**." (Hosea 13:4)*

Christianity digressed from the concept of the Oneness of God and adopted the confusing doctrine of the trinity that continues to be a source of controversy within the Christian religion. The doctrine of the Trinity states that God is the union of three divine persons - the Father, the Son and the Holy Spirit. Deviating from truth and started wandering away.

When this practice of the Trinity Doctrine began, it concealed the "Name of Jesus" from being applied in Baptism. The name of JESUS is so powerful because by this name we are saved:

Neither is there salvation in any other name but JESUS:

> *Neither is there salvation in any other: for there is **none other name** under heaven given among men, whereby we must be saved. (Acts4:12)*

There were Jewish and Gentile Christians who would not take on this baptism of the titles (Father, Son and Holy Spirit). The church age went into Apostasy. (What it meant? falling away from the truth).

Apostasy is a rebellion against God because it is a rebellion against truth.

Let's compare what the NASB and the KJV bibles say on this important matter.

Underlined sentence is removed from the NIV, NASB, and other translations of The Bible.

*"Let no one in any way deceive you, for it [Jesus' return] will not
come unless the **apostasy** comes first, and the man of lawlessness is
revealed, the son of destruction," (2 Thessalonians 2:3 **NASB Version**)*

*"Let no man deceive you by any means: for that day (Jesus' return)
shall not come, **except there comes a falling away first**, and that man
of sin be revealed, the son of perdition;"
(2 Thessalonians 2:3 **KJ Version**)*

The stewardess was very interested in what I was teaching her. However,
in view of time constraints, I explained the Oneness of God to give her a
full understanding in the brief time I had.

*"Beware lest any man spoil you through philosophy and vain deceit,
after the tradition of men, after the rudiments of the world, and not
after Christ.*

*For in him dwelleth all the fullness of the Godhead bodily."
(Colossians 2:8-9)*

Satan's Seat (Also known as Pergamos, Pergos or Pergemon):

I also explained to the Stewardess the key-role that the country of Turkey
plays in our modern day and end time. Pergamon or Pergamum was an
ancient Greek city in modern-day Turkey that became the capital of the
Kingdom of Pergamon during the Hellenistic period under the Attalid
dynasty, 281-133 BC. The city stands on a hill where you will find the
Temple of their chief God Asclepius. There is a statue of Asclepius
seated holding a staff with a serpent curling itself around it. The Book of
Revelation talks about Pergamum, one of the Seven Churches. John of
Patmos referred to it as "Satan's Seat" in his Book of Revelation.

*"And to the angel of the church in Pergamos write; These things saith
he which hath the sharp sword with two edges; I know thy works, and
where thou dwellest, even where **Satan's seat** is: and thou holdest fast*

my name, and hast not denied my faith, even in those days wherein Antipas was my faithful martyr, who was slain among you, where Satan dwelleth. But I have a few things against thee, because thou hast there them that hold the doctrine of Balaam, who taught Balac to cast a stumblingblock before the children of Israel, to eat things sacrificed unto idols, and to commit fornication." (Revelation 2:12-14)

Why is this city so important today? The reason is when Cyrus the Great, took over Babylon in 457 B.C., King Cyrus enforced the pagan Babylonian priesthood to flee westward to PERGAMOS in present day Turkey.

{Note: We need to look to Israel and the fulfillment of prophecy. Is it no wonder that on July 6, 2010, in Madrid Spain, that Syrian President Assad warned that Israel and Turkey are near at war? God's beloved Israel and Satan's (Seat) Throne coming together in today's news

After discussing Pergamos with the airline hostess, I began teaching about the New Birth. She had never heard anyone speak in tongues (Holy Ghost). I gave her all the information, scriptures and a list of where she could find a Bible believing church. She was so excited about this truth and revelation. Now I understood why I had unexplainably purchased a non-direct flight to California. God always knows what He is doing and I learned that I don't always know his intent but can later look back and see that He had a plan all along. As soon as I arrived in California, I walked off the airplane pain free and without fever.

The Question: What is Apostolic?

I was on another flight from Dallas-Ft. Worth to Ontario, California. After taking a short nap I noticed the lady next to me was reading. She was trying to look outside with some difficulty, so I lifted the blind to my window and she was happy. I was looking for an opportunity to talk with her so this gesture began our conversation that lasted nearly an hour. I began telling her about my testimony.

She said that she would view it when she checked into her hotel room. We began talking about church when she confessed that she only went once in a while. She also told me she was married and had two daughters. I then told her that I went to an Apostolic Pentecostal Church. This is when I noted her eyes opened wide. She told me that recently she and her husband had seen a billboard about an Apostolic Church. We did not know what that word (Apostolic) meant, she said. I explained to her that this was the doctrine established by Jesus in John 3:5 and applied in the Book of Acts describing the early church of the apostolic age. I firmly believe that God put me next to this lady to answer this very question. It was too much of a coincidence to be by chance.

Apostolic Age:

It is assumed that Christ was born before BC 4 or after 6 AD and was crucified between AD 30 and AD 36, at the age of 33. Thus, the founding of the Christian Church was estimated to be on the feast of Pentecost in May AD 30.

The Apostolic Age covers about seventy years (30 – 100 AD) extending from the Day of Pentecost to the death of the Apostle John.

From the writing of the epistles of John, the first century was drifting away from truth. Darkness entered the churches in the first century. Apart from that, we know very little about this period of church history. The book of Acts (2:41) records the Pentecostal conversion of three thousand people in one day at Jerusalem. History says Mass murder under Nero. The Christian converts were for the most part from the middle and lower class people, such as the illiterate, slaves, traders, and etc. It is estimated that, at the time of the conversion of Constantine, the number of Christians under this Roman decree may have reached over eleven millions, one-tenth of the total population of the Roman Empire which is a massive and fast success for Christianity. This resulted in cruel treatment of Christians living in a hostile world.

Jesus taught that we should love one another as ourselves and that salvation and repentance of sin would come in His name.

And that repentance and remission of sins should be preached in his name among all nations, beginning at Jerusalem. (Luke 24:47)

The apostles took the teachings of Jesus and applied them on the Day of Pentecost, then went out preaching Jesus to the Jews first, then to the Gentiles.

*"Take heed therefore unto yourselves, and to all the flock, over the which the Holy Ghost hath made you overseers, **to feed the church of God, which he hath purchased with his own blood**. For I know this, that after my departing shall grievous wolves enter in among you, not sparing the flock. Also of your own selves shall men arise, speaking perverse things, to draw away disciples after them. Therefore, watch, and remember, that by the space of three years I ceased not to warn every one night and day with tears." (Acts 20:28-31)*

Not everyone submitted to the Roman Empire decree of Constantine.

There were those that followed the original teaching of the Apostles, who would not accept the "conversion" laid out in the decree of Constantine. The decree included the religious traditions that were made up during the Roman Church Councils along with changes that were made that twisted the truth of the early church. These people who made up the councils that designed the decree of Constantine were not true born again believers.

This is why many churches today call themselves Apostolic or Pentecostal, following the teachings of the Apostles.

"Not many wise after the flesh, not many mighty, not many noble were called, but God chose the foolish things of the world, that he might put to shame them that are wise; and God chose the weak things of the world that he might put to shame the things that are strong; and the base things of the world, and the things that are despised, did God

choose, yea, and the things that are not, that he might bring to naught the things that are: that no flesh should glory before God."
(1 Cor. 1:26-29)

Inter-faith

Today we have a new threat against the principles of God. It is called "Interfaith." "Interfaith states that giving respect to **all gods** is important. Divided loyalty and divided reverence are acceptable to inter-faithers. We can have respect for one another as individuals and love one another, even when we disagree; however, the Bible is clear as crystal about the "Jealousy of God" that demands exclusive devotion to Him and giving reverence to other gods is a snare.

"Take heed to thyself, lest thou make a covenant with the inhabitants of the land whither thou goest, lest it be for a snare in the midst of thee: But ye shall destroy their altars, break their images, and cut down their groves: For thou shalt worship no other god: for the LORD, whose name is Jealous, is a jealous God: Lest thou make a covenant with the inhabitants of the land, and they go a whoring after their gods, and do sacrifice unto their gods, and one call thee, and thou eat of his sacrifice;" **(Exodus 34:12-15)**

The devil has come up with the deceptive belief of "Inter- faith" to fool the very elect. He knows how to manipulate modern- man with his own device of political correctness when in fact a covenant is being made by acknowledging or giving reverence to their false gods, idols and images.

Chapter 18

Ministry In Mumbai, India
"A Man Of Great Faith"

S ometime prior to 1980, I went to Mumbai India to get a visa in order to travel outside of the country. As I traveled through Mumbai by train, I noticed that we were going through a slum area of very poor people and huts. I had never seen such deplorable living conditions with people living in horrendous poverty.

I stated in the beginning that I was raised in a strict religious family. My father was a doctor and my mother was a nurse. Although we were religious and I read much of the Bible, I did not have the Holy Ghost during that time in my life. My heart was grieved as the burden of the Lord came upon me. From that day forward, I carried this burden for these people who were without hope in these slums. I didn't want anyone to see my tears, so I put my head down hiding my face. I just wanted to fall asleep but my burden for these people felt as though it was bigger than a nation. I prayed asking God, "Who will go to preach the gospel to these people?" I was thinking that I would be afraid to come to this area myself. I did not understand at that time that God's hand was so big that He could reach anyone, anywhere. Little did I know then, that God would bring me back to this place in the years to come. Back in America, and

12 years later, my burden for the people living in the slums of Mumbai was still in my heart.

Indian custom, and that of our family, was to always receive ministers into our home, feed them, supply their needs and give them a donation. I used to be a Methodist, but now I had received the revelation of the truth and there was no compromise. My family was expecting an Indian minister who was visiting in America to arrive. We waited but he did not arrive on time. I had to go to work and missed the opportunity to meet him but my mom later told me that he was very genuine. The following year, 1993, the same minister came to our home in West Covina, California for a second time. This time my brother told him that he needed to meet his sister because she was true to the Word of God and the family respected her faith and belief in God. This was the day I met Pastor Chacko. We began to discuss baptism and his belief of the Word of God. Pastor Chacko told me that he baptized in full submersion in the name of Jesus and that he would not compromise with any other kind of baptism. I was very pleased and excited to know that this man of God was doing it the Biblical way of the apostolic early church. He then extended an invitation for me to visit Mumbai, India where he lives.

I told my pastor about Pastor Chacko's strong conviction of the Word of God and his visit to our home. That evening, Pastor Chacko came to visit our church, my pastor asked him to say a few words before the congregation. There was great interest in the work that Pastor Chacko was doing in Mumbai that my church started supporting him financially and with our prayers. Our church was mission minded. We always paid Mission as we pay Tithes. This was amazing how everything began to fall into place and Mumbai now had support from my local church in California.

The following year, God sent me to India, so I accepted Pastor Chaco's offer to visit the church and his family in Mumbai. When I first arrived, pastor Chacko came to pick me up from the airport. He took me to my hotel. It was also where they met for church and in the same slum that I had passed through by train in 1980. It was now 1996 and my heartfelt prayer of hope for these beautiful souls was answered. Pastor Chacko was very hospitable and shared with me his burden and desire to build a church. I was able to visit other churches and was asked to speak before the congregation before leaving to my city of destination, Ahmadabad. I was so sadden about the living conditions of the church in Mumbai. A Catholic father gave a class room to Pastor Chacko for Sunday service.

People were so very poor, but I had the joy of witnessing the small beautiful children that were praising and serving God. They ate together with only a small piece of bread that was passed and water to drink. I was moved with compassion to buy them food and asked them to give me a list of things they needed. I did whatever I could to meet the needs on that list. They graced me with their prayers after my long flight to India. A brother from the church prayed over me and I felt the power of the Holy Ghost like electricity come instantly over my weakened and sleepless body. I felt refreshed as strength returned and my pain was gone throughout my body. Their prayers were so powerful that I was blessed beyond anything I can explain. They gave me more than what I had given them. Before flying back to America, I left Ahmadabad and returned to Mumbai, to visit Pastor Chacko one more time. I gave him all the rupees that I had left as a donation for him and his family.

Thankfully, he testified to me about his wife who was gravely ashamed when walking by the store where they owed money. She walked with her head shamefully looking down because they were unable to pay this debt. Pastor Chacko also told me about his son's education. Fees owed to the school were due and his son would not be able to continue school. I could see that the situation was overwhelming for the family. God had moved me to give and the donation I had given was more than sufficient to take care of both matters and abundantly more. Praise God!

"Defend the poor and fatherless: do justice to the afflicted and needy.
Deliver the poor and needy, rid them out of the hand of the wicked."
(Psalms 82:3-4)

When I returned to California, I prayed and cried about this small church and its people. I was so broken that I asked God about the agreement of two or three on touching anything they ask.

"Verily I say unto you, whatsoever ye shall bind on earth shall be bound in heaven: and whatsoever ye shall loose on earth shall be loosed in heaven. Again I say unto you, that if two of you shall agree on earth as touching anything that they shall ask, it shall be done for them of my Father which is in heaven. For where two or three are gathered together in my name, there am I in the midst of them."
(Matthew 18:18-20)

It was my burden and my concern to help God's church in Mumbai but I needed to share my burden with someone. One day my co-worker, Karen, asked me how I could pray for such a long time? I asked Karen if she would also like to learn how to pray longer periods, building her prayer life and fast with me. She graciously agreed and became my prayer partner. Karen also shared in my burden for Mumbai. As we began praying and fasting, she became eager to pray longer periods and fast more. She was not going to any church at the time but was very serious and sincere in what she was doing spiritually. We prayed during our lunch periods and after work we met to pray for 1½ hour in the car. A few months later, Karen told me that she had come into some money from insurance because her uncle had passed away. Karen is very kindhearted and a giver, and said that she wanted to pay tithes from this money by giving it to the ministry in Mumbai. The money was sent to Pastor Chacko to purchase a facility where they can have their own Church. They purchased a small room that had been used for Satanic Worship. They cleaned it up and restored it to their church. The following year Karen and I went to Mumbai for the dedication of the church. It was a prayer answered, for Karen who is now serving the Lord is strong in the faith. Praise God!

As the church in Mumbai was growing, Pastor Chacko requested help with a donation to purchase a small lot next to the church. Pastor Chacko had great faith for the growth of the church and for the work of God. This land belonged to the Catholic Church. Pastor Chacko and the priest had an amicable relationship and the priest was willing this lot to sell to Pastor Chacko. Pastor Chacko did not receive the donation that he believed God would provide. God knows everything and He does things His way and better than we can even imagine!

A few years later there were rioting between the Hindus and the Christian all over India. Hindus were trying to get rid of the Christians from India. The rioters came into the church during the morning with the police in support of them. They began destroying the church but Pastor Chacko and church members begged them not to for their own sakes because this was a dangerous thing for them to destroy the House of Almighty God. The rioters continued to destroy everything in sight, not heeding the warnings and pleading of the people until the church was completely demolished. The rest of the day, the church members were afraid of this very notorious and vicious group because they knew their own lives were in danger.

They felt the sadness of not having their church anymore after having prayed so long to have a place of their own to worship God. This was the place where they saw God perform miracles, demons were cast out, and salvation preached to the sinner. That very night at approximately midnight, there was a knock at Pastor Chacko's door. Fear struck him when he saw that it was the leader of this notorious group that earlier destroyed the church. Pastor Chacko thought he would be killed for certain and it was his end. He prayed asking God to give him courage to open the door and for protection. When he opened the door, to his surprise, he saw the man with tears in his eyes asking Pastor Chacko to forgive them for what they had done earlier that day to his church.

The man continued to tell Pastor Chacko that after the destruction of the church, the wife of the leader had died. One of the rioters had his hand cut off by a machine. Things were coming against the people who destroyed the church. There was fear among the rioters for what they had done against Pastor Chacko's and his God! God said He would fight our battles and so he did. Religious Hindus and Christians in India are God fearing people that will do anything to make things right. Because of what was happening to the Hindus for partaking in the destruction of the church, the same rioters returned to re-build the church out of fear. They also took possession of the property that belonged to the Catholic Church. No one came against them or complained. The rioters themselves rebuilt the church, provided the materials and all of the labor without the help of the church. When the church was completed, it was larger with two stories instead of one.

God answered Pastor Chacko's prayer and he says, "Jesus never fails." We have continued to pray for Mumbai. Today there are 52 churches, an orphanage, and two day care centers, thanks to the faith and prayers of many who have a burden for India. I began to think about how my heart had been deeply touched while I was on that train back in 1980. Little did I know that God had His eyes on this part of my country and brought love and hope to the people of the slums of Mumbai through unfailing prayers and a God that listens to the heart. In the beginning, I said that my burden was as big as a nation. I appreciate God for giving me this burden. God is the great strategist. It did not happen instantly, but through the course of sixteen years, things were happening unknown to me, as He was laying down the foundation for results to answered prayer, all while I lived in America.

The Bible says pray without ceasing. I prayed consistently and fasted for revival all over India. My country was going through a spiritual metamorphosis for the Lord Jesus.

Pastor Chacko's website is: http://www.cjcindia.org/index.html

Chapter 19

Ministry in Gujarat!

I In the late 1990s, I visited the city of Ahmedabad, in the state of Gujarat. During my last visit to Mumbai, India, I felt a sense of accomplishment for the work there. Later that trip, I visited the city of Ahmedabad and witnessed. I knew most of the people were Trinitarian. All my contacts were Trinitarians. I prayed for many years to bring this truth to the country of India. My first prayer was, I want to win someone like Paul or Peter, so my work would become easier and continue. I always pray with a plan and vision. Before I visit any place, I pray and fast, especially going to India. I always pray and fast for three days and nights without food or water or until I am Spirit-filled. This is the Biblical way of fasting.

Esther 4:16 Go, gather together all the Jews that are present in Shushan, and fast ye for me, and neither eat nor drink three days, night or day: I also and my maidens will fast likewise; and so will I go in unto the king, which is not according to the law: and if I perish, I perish.

Jonah 3:5 So the people of Nineveh believed God, and proclaimed a fast, and put on sackcloth, from the greatest of them even to the least of them. 6 For word came unto the king of Nineveh, and he arose from his throne, and he laid his robe from him, and covered him with sackcloth, and sat in ashes.7 And he caused it to be proclaimed and published through Nineveh by the decree of the king and his nobles, saying, Let neither man nor beast, herd nor flock, taste any thing: let them not feed, nor drink water:

India has been consumed with spiritual darkness. You wouldn't dare to go there unless you were full of God's Spirit. Some years back, in the 1990s, they introduced me to Bro. Christian at some Trinitarian divinity college campus. During that visit, I was attacked by most of the trinity pastors. It was my first meeting with Brother Christian. Instead of saying praise the Lord! I asked him, "What do you preach"? "Do you baptize in the Name of Jesus"? He said, "Yes". I wanted to know how he came to know this truth. So he said, God, revealed the truth while I was worshiping God one early morning at the place called Malek Saben Stadium. God clearly spoke to me about Jesus' Name Baptism'.

During this visit, I printed and passed out over a few thousand booklets explaining the water baptism in Jesus. That made the religious church authorities angry. Religious leaders started preaching against me. They said, "Absolutely, kick her out of your house. No matter where I would go, they all would speak against me. Truth makes the devil angry, but the word of God says, 'and you will know the truth and the truth will set you free'. Meeting Bro. Christian helped me to spread the truth. Praise God for sending a oneness pastor who would teach and preach the true gospel to India.

After this visit to India in the year 1999, I became disabled and I could not go back to India. But the work was **being established**. Soon all those people who spoke against me forgot about me and now have passed away. During this physical disability time, I recorded all of Search for Truth, oneness, and doctrinal CDs and gave them away for free. I was in a wheelchair and lost my memory, so I expanded my ministry by recording books. It was hard to sit, but with the help of the Lord, I did what I couldn't physically. Depending on the Lord, will take you to the new roads and highways. We face all challenges. The Power of God is awesome that nothing can stop the anointing. The message that was fought so hard was now playing in the homes on recorded CDs. Praise

God! It was to my joy and amazement that many people knew about the Biblical doctrine and the oneness of God.

I had prayed and fasted for many years so that India would have a love for the truth. Also, it would preach freely the Gospel of Jesus in each state of India. I had a strong desire to bring knowledge of truth to them through the translation of Bible studies from the English language to Gujarati. Gujarati is the spoken language in this state. I found translators in India who were eager to help me with the translation of these Bible studies. One such translator, being a pastor himself, wanted to change the scripture from the biblical baptism of the apostolic early church by omitting the name of JESUS to Father, Son, and Holy Spirit. That is the title of One true God. It became difficult to trust my translator to keep the Word of God accurate. The Bible clearly warns us not to add or take away from the Holy Scriptures. From the Old Testament to the New Testament, we must not change the Word of God on man's interpretation. We must follow the examples of Jesus and the doctrine of apostles and prophets only.

Ephesians 2:20 And are built upon the foundation of the apostles and prophets, Jesus Christ himself being the chief corner stone;

It was the disciples who went forth preaching and teaching the Gospel of Jesus. We must follow the apostle's teaching and believe that the Bible is the infallible and authoritative Word of God.

Deuteronomy 4:1 Now therefore hearken, O Israel, unto the statutes and unto the judgments, which I teach you, for to do them, that ye may live, and go in and possess the land which the Lord God of your fathers giveth you. 2 Ye shall not add unto the word which I command you, neither shall ye diminish ought from it, that ye may keep the commandments of the Lord your God which I command you.

I choose to state here that there is a big difference between what we believe to be the truth today and what the early church was teaching. Even during early church history, there were some already turning away from sound doctrine according to Paul's letters to the churches. Many versions of the Bible have changed to fit the devil's doctrine. I preferred the KJV since it is a 99.98% accurate translation close to the original scrolls.

Carefully read and examine the following scriptures:

2 Peter 2:1 But there were false prophets also among the people, even as there shall be false teachers among you, who privily shall bring in damnable heresies, even denying the Lord that bought them, and bring upon themselves swift destruction. 2 And many shall follow their pernicious ways; by reason of whom the way of truth shall be evil spoken of. 3 And through covetousness shall they with feigned words make merchandise of you: whose judgment now of a long time lingereth not, and their damnation slumbereth not.

Having the revelation of Jesus's identity, it gave apostle Peter the keys to the Kingdom and preached his first sermon on the day of Pentecost. They warned us about deceivers who have a form of godliness and do not follow the doctrine of apostles and prophets. One God believer cannot be Antichrist since they knew Jehovah will come in flesh one day.

2 John 1:7 For many deceivers are entered into the world, who confess not that Jesus Christ is come in the flesh. This is a deceiver and an antichrist. 8 Look to yourselves, that we lose not those things which we have wrought, but that we receive a full reward. 9 Whosoever transgresseth, and abideth not in the doctrine of Christ, hath not God. He that abideth in the doctrine of Christ, he hath both the Father and the Son. 10 If there come any unto you, and bring not this doctrine, receive him not into your house, neither bid him God speed: 11 For he that biddeth him God speed is partaker of his evil deeds.

There were many conferences in India where preachers went from Stockton Bible college and other states to deliver the message of being born again. Rev. McCoy, who had a calling to preach in India, did a wonderful job preaching to many places in India. With many hours of prayer and fasting, the success of the Indian ministry has continued since the year 2000. I remembered calling one minister, Pastor Miller, whom

Foreign Mission Asia Director had referred me to. When I called him at his home, he told me he was about to call me to let me know he had been in Calcutta and West Bengal six months before. He also wanted to go to Ahmedabad, but because of illness, he returned to America. Pastor Miller graciously said he wanted to go back to India but had to pray about it and asked God if his calling was for this country. He returned for the second time to India and preached at two general conferences. As God was moving mightily with the Gujarati people of this state.

Pastor Christian said it was very difficult to establish the work of God in this state. Please pray for the preachers who are facing an enormous battle. The Lord is doing great work in the state of Gujarat. The devil is not fighting against the unbelievers because he already got them! He is attacking those who have the truth; the faithful chosen of the Lord. Jesus paid the price with His blood so that we may have remission or forgiveness of our sins. The devil will fight even stronger against the ministry (Ministers) by attacking both men and women. Devil uses any perverted means to bring them to a fallen state of sin and condemnation.

John 15:16 Ye have not chosen me, but I have chosen you, and ordained you, that ye should go and bring forth fruit, and that your fruit should remain: that whatsoever ye shall ask of the Father in my name, he may give it you.

Once saved, always saved is also another lie of the devil. Between 1980 to 2015, I visited India a few times. Many changes had taken place in this nation. When you start a work of God, remember you're making disciples of Jesus, which is the continuation of the work started by Jesus and His disciples. We would have won the world by now if we continued following the Gospel of Jesus Christ.

In the year 2013, according to the plan of God, He moved me to a church in Dallas, Tax. I was sitting under the true prophet of God. He had nine gifts from the Spirit of God. He gets the knowledge of your name, address, phone number, etc. accurately by the Holy Spirit. It was new to me. In the year 2015, one Sunday morning, my pastor in Dallas, Texas, looked at me and said, I see an Angel opening a big door that no man can shut. He called me out and asked, are you going to the Philippines? He said I saw neither black nor white people there. As receiving further information from the Holy Spirit, he then asked are you going to India? The Holy Spirit spoke to him, saying I will minister to the Hindus. During that time, Christians in India were in danger. The Hindus were attacking Christians by burning their sanctuary and beating pastors and saints of Jesus up.

I believe in the prophecy, so I obeyed the voice of God and went to India. When I reached Badlapur college, 98% of the students were Hindus who converted to Christianity. It amazed me to hear their testimonies about how God is bringing people out of the darkness to light. Through their testimonies, I learned a lot about Hinduism. It amazed me to hear that they believe in 33 million and more gods and goddesses. I couldn't understand how one can believe there are so many gods and goddesses.

In 2015, I returned to Badlapur, Bombay after 23 years to teach at the Bible college. I minister there to the Bible college translator, brother Sunil. Brother Sunil was in a transitional mode. Br. Sunil was discouraged, not knowing that God was changing his direction and was discouraged. While working with him, I knew he had the truth and a love for it. Never deviate from the truth of the Bible. Let the Holy Spirit lead, guide, teach, and empower you to witness miracles and healings. India still needs many laborers, true prophets, and teachers. Please pray that God sends many laborers to India.

During this mission trip, I visited a city called Vyara in South Gujarat. I heard of a great revival going on in South Gujarat. God opened the door for me to visit there. I was very excited to be there, and I met many idol worshipers which are now turning to the one true God. This is because they received healing, deliverance, and salvation through the name of Jesus. How great our God is!

Many people are praying and fasting for India. Please pray for a revival. During the visit to Vyara, the pastor invited me to his home. I prayed over him and many of the hindering spirits broke off. After that, he was free from worry, doubt, heaviness, and fear. God prophesied through me to build a house for prayer. The pastor said we have no money. God told me He will provide. Within a year, they had a big beautiful prayer place, and we paid it off. God's word does not come back void.

During my last visit in 2015 to India, I ministered to many Hindus who converted to Christianity in different states. I also ministered to many non-Christians who experienced the signs and wonders done in the Name of Jesus and amazed. I saw many years of prayer with fasting answers for India. Praise God! Since I received the revelation of this truth, I have been working nonstop to provide this information through CDs, audio, video, YouTube channel, and books for the country of India. Our hard work is not in vain!

Later, I heard that brother Sunil accepted his calling as a pastor for Bombay and the surrounding cities. Now I am working with Pastor Sunil and other places I visited in 2015. We have established many sanctuaries in the state of Maharashtra and Gujarat. Even today, I continue to discipling the new converts in those states. I supporting them through prayers and teaching. I support financially the work of God in India.

Many of these people go to witch doctors when they are sick, but they are not getting healed. So they call me every morning and I minister, pray and cast the demons out in Jesus' name. They are being healed and delivered in Jesus' name. We have many new converts in different states. As they are being healed and delivered, they go out to testify to their families, friends, and to their villages to bring others to Christ. Many of them ask me to send a picture of Jesus. They said we would like to see God, who heals, delivers sets free, and gives salvation free. God's work can continue if we have laborers. Many of them work on the farm. Many are illiterate, so they listen to the recordings of the New Testament and Bible studies. This helps them to know and learn about Jesus.

On my last Saturday in November 2015 in India, I came home late from ministering. I was determined to stay home on Sunday and Monday to pack and prepare for my further journey to the UAE. As the pastor in Dallas Prophesied over me, 'I saw an Angel opening an enormous door that no one can close.' It proved that even I could not close that door.

Late that Saturday night, I received a phone call inviting me to attend the Sunday worship services but it wouldn't fit into my schedule so I tried to explain this to them but they wouldn't take NO for an answer. I have no choice but to go. The next morning, they dropped me off at the sanctuary at 9 am, but it starts at 10 am. I was by myself and a musician was practicing his songs.

As I was praying, I saw many spirits of the Hindu gods and goddesses in the sanctuary. I wondered why there were so many of them in this place. Around 10 o'clock, the pastor and the members started arriving. They were greeting me by shaking my hand. When the Pastor shook my hand, instantly I felt funny in my heart. I felt I was going to collapse. Later, the Holy Spirit told me that the pastor was under attack by those demons you saw earlier. I started praying and asking God to allow me to minister to this pastor. In the middle of the service, they asked me to come up and speak. While walking toward the pulpit, I prayed and asked the Lord to speak through me. As I got the microphone, I explained what God showed me and what was happening to the pastor. As the pastor knelt, I asked the congregation to stretch forth their hand toward him to pray. Meanwhile, I laid my hand on him and prayed and all the demons left. He testified he was in the emergency room the previous night. He had been fasting and praying for young people. That was why he was under this attack. Glory to God! How important it is to be in tune with the Spirit of God! His spirit speaketh to us.

From there, I went to the UAE on the 1st of December 2015. I ministered in Dubai and Abu Dhabi to the Hindu people and they also experienced the power of God. After completing my assignment, I returned to Dallas, Texas.

Praise God!

My YouTube Channels:Daily Spiritual Diet:

1. youtube.com/@dailyspiritualdietelizabet7777/videos
2. youtube.com/@newtestamentkjv9666/videos mp3
3. Website: https://waytoheavenministry.org

Chapter 20

Shepherd Of Our Soul: The Sound Of The Trumpet

I am the good shepherd, and know my sheep, and am known of mine.
(John 10:14)

Jesus is the Shepherd of our soul. We are flesh and blood with a living soul. We are on this earth but for a moment in God's time. In a moment, in a twinkling of an eye, it will all be over with the sound of the "Trumpet" when we will be changed.

"But I would not have you to be ignorant, brethren, concerning them which are asleep, that ye sorrow not, even as others which have no hope. For if we believe that Jesus died and rose again, even so them also which sleep in Jesus will God bring with him. For this we say unto you by the word of the Lord, that we which are alive and remain unto the coming of the Lord shall not prevent them which are asleep. For the Lord himself shall descend from heaven with a shout, with the voice of the archangel, and with the trump of God: and the dead in Christ shall rise first: Then we which are alive and remain shall be caught up together with them in the clouds, to meet the Lord in the air: and so

shall we ever be with the Lord. Wherefore comfort one another with these words." (1 Thessalonians 4:13-18)

Only those who have the Spirit of God (Holy Ghost) will be quickened and raised to be with the Lord. The dead in Christ will be called up first then those that are alive will be caught up in the air to meet Our Lord Jesus in the clouds. Our mortal bodies will be changed to be with the Lord. When the time of the Gentiles is fulfilled, those without the Holy Ghost will be left behind to face a time of great sorrow and tribulation.

"But in those days, after that tribulation, the sun shall be darkened, and the moon shall not give her light, And the stars of heaven shall fall, and the powers that are in heaven shall be shaken. And then shall they see the Son of man coming in the clouds with great power and glory. And then shall he send his angels, and shall gather together his elect from the four winds, from the uttermost part of the earth to the uttermost part of heaven." (Mark 13:24-27)

Many will be lost because they did not have the fear (respect) of God to believe in His Word that they might be saved. The fear of the Lord is the beginning of wisdom. King David wrote, "The LORD is my light and my salvation; whom shall I fear? The LORD is the strength of my life; of whom shall I be afraid? David was truly a man after God's heart. When God formed man of the dust of the ground He breath into his nostrils the breath of life and man became a living soul. The battle is over the soul; one's soul could be heading for God or for hell.

*"And fear not them which kill the body, but are not able to kill the **soul**: but rather fear him which is able to destroy both soul and body in **hell**." (Matthew 10:28)*

Many will know on that day, what was too difficult for them to accept today. It will be too late to turn back the pages of life as many will stand before the Living God to give an account.

129

Elizabeth Das

> _"Now this I say, brethren, that flesh and blood cannot inherit the kingdom of God; neither doth corruption inherit incorruption. Behold, I shew you a mystery; We shall not all sleep, but we shall all be changed, In a moment, in the twinkling of an eye, at the last trump: for the trumpet shall sound, and the dead shall be raised incorruptible, and we shall be changed. For this corruptible must put on incorruption, and this mortal must put on immortality. So when this corruptible shall have put on incorruption, and this mortal shall have put on immortality, then shall be brought to pass the saying that is written, Death is swallowed up in victory. O death, where is thy sting? O grave, where is thy victory? The sting of death is sin; and the strength of sin is the law. But thanks be to God, which giveth us the victory through our Lord Jesus Christ." (I Corinthians 15:50-57)_

What will we be "saved" from? An Eternal Hell in a lake that burns with fire. We are taking souls away from the clutches of the devil. This is a Spiritual Warfare that we are fighting on this earth. We will be judged by the Word of God, (66 books of the Bible), and the Book of Life will be opened.

> _"And I saw a great white throne, and him that sat on it, from whose face the earth and the heaven fled away; and there was found no place for them. And I saw the dead, small and great, stand before God; and the books were opened: and another book was opened, which is the book of life: and the dead were judged out of those things which were written in the books, according to their works. And the sea gave up the dead which were in it; and death and hell delivered up the dead which were in them: and they were judged every man according to their works. And death and hell were cast into the lake of fire. This is the second death. And whosoever was not found written in the book of life was cast into the lake of fire." (Revelations 20:11-15)_

I began to think about men such as Moses, King David, Joseph, Job and the list goes on. I did not enjoy all the pain I experienced and I don't understand why there is such suffering in Christianity. I am far from being like these men that are our examples and who bring us inspiration to walk the walk of faith. God's Word prevails even in the middle of suffering and pain. In the time of trial, sickness, and distress, we call upon God the most. It is a strange but wonderful faith, that only God knows why He has chosen this way. He loves us so much, and yet He has given us the ability to choose for ourselves whether we will serve and love Him. He is looking for a passionate bride. Would you marry someone who was not passionate about you? This chapter is written as encouragement to overcome those things that will hinder you from attaining everlasting life. The God of Love, Mercy and Grace will become the God of judgment. Now is the time to make your salvation sure and escape the flames of hell. We must choose as Joshua chose in the book of Joshua.

And if it seem evil unto you to serve the LORD, choose you this day whom ye will serve; whether the gods which your fathers served that were on the other side of the flood, or the gods of the Amorites, in whose land ye dwell: but as for me and my house, we will serve the LORD. (Joshua 24:15)

"And, behold, I come quickly; and my reward is with me, to give every man according as his work shall be. I am Alpha and Omega, the beginning and the end, the first and the last. Blessed are they that do his commandments, that they may have right to the tree of life, and may enter in through the gates into the city." (Revelation 22:12-14)

Everyone wants to go through the gates into the City that God has prepared for us but, we must have a garment spotless and without blemish before we may enter. This is spiritual warfare, "fought and won" on our knees in prayer. We only have one life on this earth and only one good fight! The only thing we can take with us to that City are the souls of those that we have witnessed to, that accepted the Gospel of Our Lord and Savior Jesus Christ, and who obeyed the doctrine of Christ. To know the Word, we must read it, to read the Word is to fall in love with the author of our Salvation. I thank my Lord and Savior for directing my steps from India to America and showing me His Ways for they are perfect.

Thy word is a lamp unto my feet, and a light unto my path.
(Psalm 119:105)

Chapter 21

Ministry At Work

Since I received the Holy Ghost, big changes came into my life.

But ye shall receive power, after that the Holy Ghost is come upon you: and ye shall be witnesses unto me both in Jerusalem, and in all Judaea, and in Samaria, and unto the uttermost part of the earth. (Acts1:8)

I tried to minster at my work to coworkers; I would witness and if they had a problem I would pray for them. Many times they would come to me and tell me their situation and I would pray over them. If they were sick, I would lay hands on them and pray for them. For many years I testified to them. My own life was being a great testimony and God was working with me, confirming through healing, deliverance, counseling and comforting them.

And he said unto them, Go ye into all the world, and preach the gospel to every creature. He that believeth and is baptized shall be saved; but he that believeth not shall be damned. And these signs shall follow them that believe; In my name shall they cast out devils; they shall speak with new tongues; They shall take up serpents; and if they drink any deadly thing, it shall not hurt them; they shall lay hands on the sick, and they shall recover. So then after the Lord had spoken unto them, he was received up into heaven, and sat on the right hand of God. And they went forth, and preached everywhere, the Lord working with them, and confirming the word with signs following. Amen. (Mark 16:15-20)

Wherever I prayed, if they were healed or delivered, I talked to them about the Gospel. The Gospel is the Death, Burial, and Resurrection of Jesus. This means, we need to repent of all sins or we die to our flesh by repenting. The second step is that we are buried in the name of Jesus in the waters of Baptism to receive remission of our sins or forgiveness of our sin. We come out of the water speaking in new tongues by receiving His spirit, which is also called the Baptism of the Spirit or the Holy Ghost.

Many heard and obeyed it too.

I would like to encourage you by giving my testimony of how Jesus worked mightily at my work place. Our work place, where we live or anywhere, is a field where we can plant the seed of the word of God.

Friend healed by cancer and her mom turn to the Lord at death bad.

I had a precious friend named Linda at my work. In the year 2000, I was very sick. One day, my friend called me and said she was also very sick and had undergone some surgery. In the beginning year of our friendship she rejected the Gospel and told me I do not want your Bible or your prayers, I have my own god. I was not hurt but whenever she complained of sickness, I would offer to pray, she would always say "No". But one day, she had an unbearable pain in her back and suddenly she had a pain in her knee also. It was an even greater pain than was in her back. She complained, and I asked if I could pray for her. She said, "Do whatever it takes". I took this opportunity to teach her how to rebuke this pain in the Name of the Lord Jesus. Her pain was unbearable; she started rebuking the pain right away in the Name of the Lord Jesus, the pain left instantly.

However, this healing did not change her heart. God uses affliction and problems to soften our heart. That is the rod of correction He uses for His children. One day Linda called me crying that she had a big cut on her neck and it was very painful. She begged me to pray. I was more than happy to pray for my good friend. She kept calling me every hour for comfort and said, "can you come to my home and pray"? That afternoon she received a phone call telling her that she was diagnosed with thyroid cancer. She cried very hard and when her mom heard that her daughter had cancer, she just collapsed. Linda was divorced and had a young son.

She insisted that I come and pray over her. I also was so hurt by hearing this report. I earnestly began looking for someone who could drive me to her house, so I could pray over her. Praise God, if there is a will then there is a way.

My prayer partner came from work and took me to her home. Linda, her mother, and her son were sitting and crying. We began to pray, and I did not feel much; however, I believed that God was going to do something. I offered to pray again. She said *"Yes, pray all night, I will not mind."* While praying the second time I saw a bright light coming from the door, even though the door was closed and my eyes were closed. I saw Jesus came through that door, and I wanted to open my eyes, but He said *"keep praying"*.

As we finished praying, Linda was smiling. I did not know what had happened for her countenance to be changed. I asked her, *"What happened?"* She said *"Liz, Jesus is the true God"*. I said, *"Yes, I have been telling you that for the past 10 years, but I want to know what happened."* She said, *"My pain is completely gone."* *"Please give me the church address, I want to be baptized."* Linda agreed to do a Bible study with me and then she was baptized. Jesus used this affliction to get her attention.

> *Look upon mine affliction and my pain; and forgive all my sins.*
> *(Psalm 25:18).*

Praise God!! Please do not give up on your loved one. Keep praying day and night, one day Jesus will answer if we faint not.

> *And let us not be weary in well doing: for in due season we shall reap,*
> *if we faint not. (Galatians 6:9)*

On her mother's death bed, Linda called me to go visit her. She pushed me in my wheel chair into her hospital room. As we ministered to her mom, she repented and cried out to the Lord Jesus for forgiveness. Next day her voice was completely gone and the third day she died.

My friend Linda is a good Christian now. Praise the Lord!!

My coworker from Vietnam:

She was a sweet lady, and always had a very beautiful spirit about her. One day she was sick, and I asked if I could pray for her. She accepted my offer right away. I prayed and she was healed. The next day, she said, "If it is not too much trouble, then pray for my dad." Her dad had been continuously sick for the past few months. I told her I was more than happy to pray for her dad. Jesus in His mercy, touched and healed him completely.

Later, I saw her sick and offered to pray again. She said, "*Do not take the trouble to pray for me*"; however, her friend who works as a mechanic in another shift needs prayer. He could not sleep day or night; this disease is called Fatal Insomnia. She continued giving me information, and was very concerned about this gentleman. The doctor had given him high doses of medicine and nothing was helping. I said, "*I am more than happy to pray.*" Every night after work, I prayed almost an hour and half for all the prayer requests and for myself. As I began to pray for this man, I noticed I was not sleeping soundly. I would suddenly hear someone clap in my ear or a loud noise that would wake me up almost every night, since I had begun to pray for him.

A few days later as I had been fasting, I came home from church and laid in my bed. Then suddenly to my surprise something came through the wall over my head and walked in my room. Thank God for the Holy Ghost. Instantly the Holy Ghost spoke through my mouth, "I bind you in the name of Jesus". I knew in the spirit that something was bound and the power was broken in the name of Jesus.

Verily I say unto you, Whatsoever ye shall bind on earth shall be bound in heaven: and whatsoever ye shall loose on earth shall be loosed in heaven. (Matthew 18:18)

I did not know what that was and later while working, the Holy Ghost started revealing what had happened. Then I knew that there were demons controlling this mechanic and not letting him sleep. I asked my friend at work to please find out about her friend's sleeping condition. Later on she came back to my work area with the mechanic. He told me he was sleeping well and wanted to thank me. I said, ***"Please thank Jesus." "He is the one who delivered you."*** Later I gave him a Bible and asked him to read and pray every day.

There were many people within their family that turned to Jesus at my work. It was a great time for me to witness to many different nationalities of people.

I will give thee thanks in the great congregation: I will praise thee among much people. (Psalm 35:18)

I will extol thee, my God, O king; and I will bless thy name forever and ever. (Psalm 145:1)

Chapter 22

Learning His Ways By Obeying His Voice

I found this beautiful truth in 1982. A couple of years later, I decided to go visit India. While I was there my friend, Dinah and I decided to go sightseeing in the city of Udaipur. At the end of the day, we went back to our hotel room we were sharing. In our room there was a picture on the wall of a false god being worshiped there in India. As you know India has many gods. The Bible speaks of the one true God and His name is Jesus.

Jesus saith unto him, I am the way, the truth, and the life: no man cometh unto the Father, but by me. (John 14:6)

All of a sudden I heard this voice tell me, *"Remove the picture from the wall."* Since I have the Holy Ghost, my thought was, *"I am not afraid of anything and nothing can harm me."* So I was disobedient to this voice and did not take the picture down.

As we were sleeping, unexpectedly, I found myself sitting in the bed; I knew an Angel had set me up. God opened my spiritual eyes and I saw an enormous black spider coming through the door. It came crawling over me, my friend, and her son. And it went toward my dress that was hanging against the wall and vanished right before my eyes. At that moment the Lord reminded me of the scripture that says to never give place to the Devil.

Neither give place to the devil. (Ephesians 4:27)

Right away I got up and took the picture down and turned it over. From that day forward, I realized that God is a Holy God. His commandments which He has given us will keep us protected and blessed, as long as we always obey and keep them.

At the time I was working, I would always come home feeling spiritually drained. One day Jesus spoke to me and told me, *"speak in tongues for half an hour, praise and worship for half an hour and put my hand over my head and speak in tongues for half an hour."* This was my daily prayer life.

One day, I came home from work after midnight. I started walking around my house praying. I came to a certain corner of my house and saw a demon with my spiritual eyes. I turned on the light and put on my glasses to see why this demon would be here? All of a sudden, I remembered earlier that day, I had covered the prints and names of the gods that were on a corn oil box. Somehow, I had missed the print of this false god. I immediately got the permanent marker and covered it up.

The Bible states, Jesus has given us the authority to bind up and cast out evil spirits. That night I used the authority, opened up the door and said to that demon, *"In the Name of Jesus, I command you to get out of my house and never return!"* The demon left instantly.

Praise God! If we do not know the Word of God we can allow demons to come into our house through magazines, newspapers, T. V., even though toys. It is very important to know what we bring into our homes.

Another example of this, I was very sick and could not walk, I had to depend on family and friends to get my groceries and to put them away. One morning I woke up and felt that someone was covering my mouth, I was bound.

I asked God why I felt this way. He showed me the symbol of the Swastika. I wondered where I am going to find this symbol. I went to the refrigerator and as soon as I opened the door, I saw the swastika symbol on a grocery item that my sister had brought the day before. I thanked God for His guidance and removed it immediately.

Trust in the LORD with all thine heart; and lean not unto thine own understanding. In all thy ways acknowledge him, and he shall direct thy paths. (Proverbs 3:5-6)

I would like to share another experience I had while visiting my home town in India. I was spending a night with a friend of mine who was an idol worshiper.

For many years I had witnessed to her about Jesus and Power. She also knew the Power of prayer and many miracles that happened in her home. She was testifying about miracles when I prayed in the name of Jesus.

While I was sleeping a noise woke me up. Across the room I saw a figure that looked like my friend. The figure was pointing at me with a mean face. Its hand started growing toward me and came within a foot of me and then vanished. This figure reappears but this time it was her little boy's face. Once again its arm started growing and pointing at me. It came one foot away from me and disappeared. I remembered the Bible says that Angels are around us.

He that dwelleth in the secret place of the most High shall abide under the shadow of the Almighty. I will say of the LORD, He is my refuge and my fortress: my God; in him will I trust. Surely he shall deliver thee from the snare of the fowler, and from the noisome pestilence. He shall cover thee with his feathers, and under his wings shalt thou trust:

his truth shall be thy shield and buckler. Thou shalt not be afraid for the terror by night; nor for the arrow that flieth by day; Nor for the pestilence that walketh in darkness; nor for the destruction that wasteth at noonday. A thousand shall fall at thy side, and ten thousand at thy right hand; but it shall not come nigh thee. Only with thine eyes shalt thou behold and see the reward of the wicked. Because thou hast made the LORD, which is my refuge, even the most High, thy habitation; There shall no evil befall thee, neither shall any plague come nigh thy dwelling. For he shall give his angels charge over thee, to keep thee in all thy ways. (Psalms 91:1-11)

When I woke up, in the morning I saw my friend and her son bowing down to the idols. And I remembered what God had shown me during the night. So I told my friend that I had a vision of earlier that night. She told me that she also had seen and felt it in her house. She asked me what the demon that I had seen looked like. I told her one form looked like her and the other like her son. She told me her and her son could not get along. She asked me what needed to be done to get rid of these demons that were tormenting her and her family. I explained to her this scripture.

The thief cometh not, but for to steal, and to kill, and to destroy: I am come that they might have life, and that they might have it more abundantly. (John 10:10)

I gave her the Bible and asked to read it out loud every day in her house especially, John 3:20 and 21.

For every one that doeth evil hateth the light, neither cometh to the light, lest his deeds should be reproved. But he that doeth truth cometh to the light, that his deeds may be made manifest, that they are wrought in God. (John 3:20-21)

I also taught her the spiritual warfare prayer in which you bind all evil spirits and loose the Holy Spirit or Angels in the Name of Jesus. I also asked her to speak the Name of Jesus and plead the Blood of Jesus in her house continuously.

A few months after this trip, I received a letter testifying, that the demons had left her house, she and her son were getting along, and they had total peace in their home.

Then he called his twelve disciples together, and gave them power and authority over all devils, and to cure diseases. And he sent them to preach the kingdom of God, and to heal the sick. (Luke 9:1, 2)

When she testified to other relatives, they became very interested in the Bible and wanted to learn more about the Lord Jesus.

My next visit to India, I met with the whole family and answered their questions. I taught them how to pray and gave them Bibles. I give God all the glory for these results.

My desire is that people would learn how to use the Name of Jesus and the Word of God as a sword against the enemy. By becoming a "born again Christian", we will have the power.

The Spirit of the Lord GOD is upon me; because the LORD hath anointed me to preach good tidings unto the meek; he hath sent me to bind up the brokenhearted, to proclaim liberty to the captives, and the opening of the prison to them that are bound; (Isaiah 61: 1)

Chapter 23

Moving On Media

In 1999 I had an injury at work and later it became worse. This injury was so severe that through the pain I lost my memory. I could not read and remember what I had read. I could not sleep for 48 hours. If I did sleep, I would wake up after a few hours because of the numbness in my hands, the pain in my back, neck, and legs. This was the fiery trial of my faith. I did not have any idea of what I was thinking. Many times I would faint and go to sleep. That is the only way I slept most of the time. I did not want to waste my time so I thought what should I do? I thought of making a CD of all my books which were already translated. I thought that if I put these entire books on audio, it would be great for this time and age.

That the trial of your faith, being much more precious than of gold that perisheth, though it be tried with fire, might be found unto praise and honour and glory at the appearing of Jesus Christ:(1 Peter1:7)

To spread this truth, I was willing to do anything. No price is greater than what Jesus paid. God in His mercy helped me to reach my goal.

No doubt it took over a year to do this. I did not have enough money to buy all the equipment, nor did I have enough knowledge to know how to record. I started using my credit card to buy what I needed for this new project. I thought since I cannot read and remember, I can just read the book out loud and make an audio CD, this way I do not need a memory to read.

Since I was going to an English church I almost forgot how to read Guajarati correctly, and I did not want to give up my language. Many times, as you know, due to health, I could not sit for days or even weeks. I would forget how to record and use my recording equipment. I would see my notes and start over again but I did not want to let it go.

One thing we must remember; the devil never gives up! We have to learn from that and never give up!

The day came when I finished my six-page booklet. To my surprised, it took one year to finish. I was so happy, I put the CD on to play, and slowly I reversed my wheel chair to hear my CD.

Suddenly as I looked, my eyes had no vision. I was so scared and said to myself, "I worked so hard in my poor health. I wish I would have taken better care of my health, now I cannot see." I did not see my kitchen, my stereo, wall, or furniture. Nothing was there except a thick white cloud. I said "I was hard on myself, now I am blind." Suddenly, in that thick white cloud in my room, I saw the Lord Jesus standing in a white robe and smiling at me. In a short time, He vanished away and I realized it was a Vision. I knew that His Shekinah glory had come down. I was so happy and realized that the Lord Jesus was pleased with my effort.

I always want to seek God for His direction, to use my time in the best way to give Him glory. No situation can stop us to perform His ministry. This CD I gave freely to people and also uploaded on my http://www.gujubible.org/web_site.htm and https://waytoheavenministry.org

Who shall separate us from the love of Christ? shall tribulation, or distress, or persecution, or famine, or nakedness, or peril, or sword? As

it is written, "For thy sake we are killed all the day long; we are accounted as sheep for the slaughter. Nay, in all these things we are more than conquerors through him that loved us. For I am persuaded, that neither death, nor life, nor angels, nor principalities, nor powers, nor things present, nor things to come, nor height, nor depth, nor any other creature, shall be able to separate us from the love of God, which is in Christ Jesus our Lord". (Roman 8:35-39)

Chapter 24

Study That Explores

Many times, I had opportunities to give Bible studies in languages other than English. While teaching them the Word of God, they were unable to find the right scripture. I always used the King James Version. But some of them had different versions and languages of the Bible.

One night I was teaching about One God, Monotheism (Mono comes from Greek word Monos and theos means God) and I was reading 1 John 5:7. When they looked for that scripture in their Bible they could not find it. Now, it was past midnight so I thought they did not understand what they were reading, and as we translated from English to their language, they said this is not in our Bible.

*For there are three that bear record in heaven, the Father, the Word, and the Holy Ghost: and these **three are one**. (1 John 5:7)*

I was shocked. So we searched for another scripture.

*(KJV) 1st Timothy 3:16, "**God** was manifest in the flesh"*

Their Bible read: "*He appeared in a body*" (all Bibles translated from the corrupted manuscript of Alexandrian have this lie. Roman Catholic Vulgate, Guajarati Bible, the NIV Bible, Spanish and other modern versions of the Bible)

{ΘC=God} in the Greek language but by removing the little line from ΘC, "God" changes {OC = "who" or "he"} to who, which has a different meaning in Greek language. It's two different words, because 'he' could mean anybody, but God is talking about Jesus Christ in flesh.

How easy it is to take away the deity of Jesus Christ?!?!

Revelation 1:8

KJV: I am Alpha and Omega, the beginning and the ending, saith the Lord, which is, and which was, and which is to come, the Almighty

NIV translation: Revelation 1:8 "I am the Alpha and the Omega," says the Lord God, "who is, and who was, and who is to come, the Almighty".

(Gujarati Bible, NIV and other translations have removed "Beginning and the ending")

Revelation 1:11

KJV: Saying, I am Alpha and Omega, the first and the last: and, What thou seest, write in a book, and send it unto the seven churches which are in Asia; unto Ephesus, and unto Smyrna, and unto Pergamos, and unto Thyatira, and unto Sardis, and unto Philadelphia, and unto Laodicea (Revelation 1:11)

NIV: Revelaion 1:11 "Write on a scroll what you see and send it to the seven churches: to Ephesus, Smyrna, Pergamum, Thyatira, Sardis, Philadelphia and Laodicea."

(Modern versions of the Bible, Guajarati and the NIV Bible all have removed <u>I am Alpha and Omega, the first and the last</u>)

I could not prove that there is 'One God' from their Bible.

My teaching was taking a long time, and with their surprise I could not provide scriptural evidence to them that there is One God from their Bible. This launched me to study in depth.

I remember Paul said: *For I know this, that after my departing shall grievous wolves enter in among you, not sparing the flock. (Acts 20:29)*

The Apostle John, who was the last surviving disciple of Christ, gave us a warning in one of his epistles:

Beloved, believe not every spirit, but try the spirits whether they are of God: because many false prophets are gone out into the world. Hereby know ye the Spirit of God: Every spirit that confesseth that Jesus Christ is come in the flesh is of God: And every spirit that confesseth not that Jesus Christ is come in the flesh is not of God: and this is that spirit of antichrist, whereof ye have heard that it should come; and even now already is it in the world. (1 John 4:1-3)

I would like to share this fact which I found, by searching the truth of corrupting the 'Word of God'.

The Alexandrian manuscript was a corrupted version of the original true Manuscript of the Bible. They removed many words like, Sodomite, hell, blood, created by Jesus Christ, Lord Jesus, Christ, Alleluia, and Jehovah, along with many other words and verses from the original manuscript.

In Alexandria Egypt, scribes, who were antichrist, did not have the revelation of the One True God because the Bible was changed from the original manuscript. This Corruption began in the first century.

At first Greek and Hebrew Bibles were written on Papyrus' Scrolls which were perishable. So they would hand write 50 copies in different countries every 200 years to preserve them another 200 years. This was practiced by our forefathers who had the true copy of the original manuscript. This same system was embraced by the Alexandrians' to preserve the corrupted manuscript as well.

In early AD's, the Bishops took the position and brought corruption progressively from the years 130 to 444 AD. They added and subtracted from the original copy of the Greek and Hebrew manuscript. All of the following Bishops would affirm they received messages directly from Jesus and should pay no attention to the apostles, disciples, prophets and teachers. And all the Bishops also claimed that they were the only enlightened ones.

Bishop Origen of Alexandria (185-254 CE): Tertullian was a corrupted bishop, who added more darkness. He died about 216 A.D. Clement took over and was Bishop of Alexandria. Cyril, bishop of Jerusalem, was born in the year 315 and died in 386 AD. Augustine, bishop of Hippo, founder of Catholicism, was born in 347 and died in 430 AD. He removed the people who truly believed in the Word of God. Chrysostom was another bishop of Constantinople, where the corrupted version was originated. He was born in 354 and died in 417 AD. St.Cyril of Alexandria was made bishop in 412 and died in 444 AD.

These bishops corrupted the true manuscript, and were rejected by our forefathers who knew the facts of where and how the original manuscript was corrupted.

This corruption started when Paul and John were still alive. The Alexandrians' ignored the word of God and in Nicaea, in the year of 325 AD; they established the doctrine of the Trinity. Nicaea is the modern day Turkey and in the Bible it's known as Pergamum.

*And to the angel of the church in **Pergamum** write; these things saith he which hath the sharp sword with two edges; I know thy works, and*

149

*where thou dwellest, even **where Satan's seat is**, And thou holdest fast my name, and hast not denied my faith, even in those days wherein Antipas was my faithful martyr, who was slain among you, where satan dwelleth. (Revelation 2:12-13.)*

Nicaea

In the year 325 AD the Oneness of God was removed by Satan and the Trinity was added and God was divided. They took out the "Jesus" name from the baptism formula by adding the Father, Son and Holy Ghost.

The thief cometh not, but for to steal, and to kill, and to destroy: I am come that they might have life, and that they might have it more abundantly (John 10:10.)

Pergamum (later called Nicaea and now is called Turkey) is a city built 1000ft above sea level. Four different gods are being worshiped around this place. The chief god was Asclepius whose symbol is a serpent.

Revelation says:

*And the great **dragon** was cast out, that old **serpent**, called the Devil, and Satan, which deceiveth the whole world: he was cast out into the earth, and his angels were cast out with him (Revelation 12:9).*

*And he laid hold on the dragon, that old **serpent**, which is the Devil, and Satan, and bound him a thousand years, (Revelation 20:2).*

In this temple there were many large size snakes; also around that area were thousands of snakes. People came to the temple of Pergamum in search of healing. Asclepius was called the god of healing, and was the chief god among the four gods. Since he was called the god of healing, at this place they introduced herbs and medicines for healing. So that he can remove the stripes and Jesus' Name for healing. His plan is to take the place of Jesus and remove Christ as Savior, for he also claimed himself to be a savior. Modern day Medical Science took the serpent Symbol from Asclepius (Serpent).

Bible says:

*Ye are my witnesses, saith the LORD, and my servant whom I have chosen: that ye may know and believe me, and understand that **I am he**: before me there was no God formed, neither shall there be after me. I, even I, am the LORD; and beside me there is no **saviour**. (Isaiah 43:10-11)*

This is the place where Satan established the trinity.

Today they have found an original copy of the Alexandria manuscript, underlining the word and scripture to remove from the original true Hebrew and Greek Manuscript. This proves that they were the ones, who corrupted the true word of God.

The Dark era came in simply by removing the truth and changing the true document of the Bible.

The word of God is a sword, light and truth. God's word is established forever and ever.

The NIV Bible, modern Bible, and many other languages of the Bible, were translated from a corrupted old Alexandria copy. Now most other copies of the Bible came from the NIV version and are translated in other languages. Satan's Bible and NIV Bibles' copy right is owned by a man named, Rupert Murdoch.

When King James took over after the virgin queen Elizabeth in 1603, he took on the project to translate the Bible from its original true Hebrew and Greek manuscript. This project was done by many Hebrew, Greek and Latin Theologians, scholars, and people who were highly respected in the eyes of others. Archaeologists have found the old true original

Hebrew and Greek manuscripts which agrees 99% with the KJV Bible. One percent is minor mistakes such as punctuation.

Praise God! The KJV is a public domain and any one can use the KJV Bible to translate it into their native language. My suggestion is that we must translate from the KJV Bible since it is public domain and is the most accurate Bible.

By removing the truth from original Bible, the name "Jesus Christ", which is the power that sets people free, was gone.

This caused the birth of many denominations. Now you will understand why the Bible says do not add to or subtract from.

The attack is on the incarnated One God.

The Bible says.

And the LORD shall be king over all the earth: in that day shall there be one LORD, and his name one. (Zechariah 14:9)

His name is JESUS!!!

Chapter 25

Life-Changing Personal Testimonials

Greetings In the Name of Jesus:

These personal "Life-Changing" testimonials are included as encouragement of the Power of Almighty God. It is my sincere hope that your faith will be increased in reading these inspirational testimonies from humble believers and ministers who have a calling and passion for God. "Know Him in the intimacy of His Love, through Faith, Prayer and the Word of God." Science and medicine cannot explain these miracles, nor can those who profess to be wise understand the things of God.

*And I will give thee the **treasures** of darkness, and hidden riches of secret places, that thou mayest know that I, the LORD, which call thee by thy name, am the God of Israel. (Isaiah 45:3)*

"This is a walk of Faith that cannot be dissected and is not imagined."

"The wise men are ashamed, they are dismayed and taken: see, they have rejected the word of the LORD and what wisdom is in them?"
(Jeremiah 8:9)

153

"Woe unto them that are wise in their own eyes, and prudent in their own sight!" (Isaiah 5:21)

"For ye see your calling, brethren, how that not many wise men after the flesh, not many mighty, not many noble, are called: But God hath chosen the foolish things of the world to confound the wise; and God hath chosen the weak things of the world to confound the things which are mighty;" (1 Corinthians 1:26-27)

Call unto me, and I will answer thee, and show thee great and mighty things, which thou knowest not. (Jeremiah 33:3)

My sincere thanks go out to those who have contributed their personal testimonies and time to this book for God's Glory.

May God Bless You
Elizabeth Das, Texas

Testimonies of the People

All Testimonies Are Given Voluntarily To Give God Glory, Glory Belongs To God Alone

Terry Baughman, Pastor
Gilbert, Arizona, U.S.A

Elizabeth Das is a woman of influence. The Apostle Paul and his missionary companion Silas were drawn to a woman' prayer group near Thyatira along the riverside. It was in this prayer meeting that Lydia heard the teaching of Paul and Silas and then insisted that they come to stay at her house during their ministry in the region. (See Acts 16:13-15.) The hospitality and... ministry of this woman is recorded in scripture to be remembered for all time.

Elizabeth Das is such a woman of God, much like the influential woman, Lydia, in the book of Acts. Through her industry and passion she has led others to the knowledge of the truth, coordinated prayer groups, and been the instrument of sending ministers of the Gospel into her homeland of Gujarat, India.The first time I heard of Elizabeth Das I was an instructor and the Academic Dean at Christian Life College in Stockton, California. Daryl Rash, our Missions Director, told me of her good work in soliciting ministers to go to Ahmadabad, India, to teach and preach in the conferences sponsored by Pastor Jaiprakash Christian and Faith Church, a group of more than 60 churches in the state of Gujarat, India. She called Christian Life College requesting speakers in an upcoming conference for the churches in India. We sent two of our instructors to provide teaching and preaching for the conference. The next time Elizabeth Das called; Daryl Rash asked me if I would like to go teach in one of the conferences. I was happy to go and immediately began preparations to make the trip. Another instructor, Brian Henry, accompanied me and preached the night services at the conference. At the time, I was the Executive Vice President of Christian Life College and a full time instructor, so we arranged substitutes for our classes and other responsibilities and flew halfway around the world to share our ministries with the wonderful people of Gujarat in Western India. On my second trip to Gujarat in 2008, my son accompanied me and he experienced a life changing event in the Spirit and Truth Conference in Anand. It is a costly endeavor to fly around the world and participate in these conferences and ministry trips, but the reward cannot be measured in monetary value. My son made a new commitment to the Lord on this trip to India that has changed the direction of his life. He is now leading worship and is the music director in the church where I now serve as pastor in Gilbert, Arizona. Not only are people blessed by the ministry in India, but also those who go there are likewise blessed, sometimes in surprising ways.

The influence of Elizabeth Das is literally being felt around the world. Not only is she instrumental in sending ministers from the United States to India, she has a passion to translate materials into Gujarati, the language of her home. Whenever I have talked with her on the phone she is constantly looking for new ways to share the truth of the Gospel. She is active in a prayer ministry and actively looks for ways to minister through Bible lessons in print and on the Internet through her YouTube recordings. Elizabeth Das is a living demonstration of what one person can do to change the world through passion, persistence, and prayer.

Veneda Ing
Milan, Tennesee, U.S.A.

I live in a small town in West Tennessee and belong to a local Pentecostal Church. A few years ago I attended a prayer conference in St. Louis, MO and met a lady named Tammy and we became instant friends. As we got to know each other she told me about a prayer group that she belonged to, led by Sister Elizabeth Das from her home in Texas. The small group included people from different parts of the United States joining in by telephone conference.

When I returned home, I began calling into the prayer group and was instantly blessed by God. I had been in church approximately 13 years when I joined this group, so prayer was not something new; however, the power of "Agreed Prayer" was astounding! I immediately began to get results on my prayer requests and listened to praise reports every day. Not only did my prayer life grow, my Jail Ministry also grew along with other gifts of the Spirit that God has blessed me with. I had never met Sister Das at this point. Her great desire to pray and to help others tap into the gifts within them always kept me coming back for more. She is very encouraging and very bold, not afraid to question things and definitely not afraid to tell you if she feels from God that something is wrong. Jesus is always her answer. When I had an opportunity to come to Texas to be a part of a special prayer meeting at Sister Das' home, I was most eager to go.

I boarded the plane and was in the Dallas-Ft. Worth Airport in just a few hours where we met for the first time of more than a year of praying together.

A familiar voice, but it seemed as though we had known each other for years. Others also came from other states to join this meeting.

The home prayer meeting was something I had never experienced before. I was so excited that God allowed me to be used to benefit others. During this meeting we saw many healed of back and neck problems. We saw and experienced legs and arms grow and witnessed someone healed of diabetes along with many other miracles and life changing events such as the casting out of demons. This just left me even more desirous of the things of God and to know Him in a higher place. Let me take a moment to stop here and interject that God performed these Miracles in the Name of Jesus and Him alone. God uses Sister Das because she is willing to help and teach others to learn how to allow God to use them as well. She is a dear friend and a mentor who has taught me to be more accountable to God. I thank God that our lives have crossed paths and we have become prayer partners. I never knew the true power of prayer in 13 years of living for God. I encourage you to form a unified prayer group and just see what God will do. He is an amazing God.

Diana Guevara
California El Monte

When I was born I was brought up in the Catholic religion of my family. I was not practicing my religion, as I got older. My name is Diana Guevara and as a little girl I always knew I should feel something when I attended church but never did. My routine was to pray the Our Father and Hail Mary, as taught to do as a small child. The truth is, I really did not know God. In February 2007 I found out that my boyfriend of 15 years was having an affair and that he was on different Internet dating sites. I was so hurt and devastated that I went into a depressive state lying on the couch crying all the time. I was so heart-stricken that I lost 25 lbs in 21 days as I felt my world had come to an end. One day I received a call from Sister Elizabeth Das, a lady I had never met. She encouraged me and prayed over me and would quote scriptures to me from the Bible. For two months we talked and she continued to pray over me and each time I felt the Peace and Love of God. In April 2007 something told me I had to go to Texas to Sister Elizabeth's home. I made my reservations and was on my way to Texas for 5 days. During this time Sis. Elizabeth and I prayed and had Bible studies. She showed me scriptures about being baptized in Jesus Name. I asked many questions about God and knew that I had to get baptized in Jesus Name as soon as possible. After I was baptized I knew then that this was the reason why I felt the urgency to go to Texas. I had finally found what I was missing as a child, the presence of Almighty God! When I returned to California I began attending Life Church.

This is where I received the gift of the Holy Ghost with the evidence of speaking in tongues. I can truly say that there is a difference between truth and religion. It was through God's love that he used Sister Elizabeth to teach me Bible studies and show me the Plan of Salvation according to the Word of God. I was born into a religion and that was all I knew without exploring the Bible for myself. Having been taught prayers to repeat, my prayers now are never routine or boring. I love to speak to the Lord. I always knew there was a God but did not know then that I could also feel His presence and His love as I do now. Not only is He present in my life, he has given me Peace and mended my heart when I thought my world had ended. The Lord Jesus has given me the Love that I was always missing in my life. I can never imagine my life without Jesus because without him I am nothing. Because He has filled the empty spaces in my heart with His love, I live for Him and Him only. Jesus is everything and He can heal your heart too. I give all The Honor and Glory to only Our Lord Jesus Christ.

Jairo Pina My Testimony

My name is Jairo Pina and I am currently 24 years of age and living in Dallas, TX. Growing up, my family and I would only go to church about once a year believing in the Catholic faith. I knew about God but did not know God. When I was 16 years of age, they diagnosed me with a malignant tumor on my right fibula known as osteosarcoma (bone cancer). I went through a year of chemotherapy and surgeries to combat this. It was during this time that I have the earliest memory of God revealing himself to me. It dragged me along to this little building in Garland, TX with a friend and his mother. My friend's mother was friends with a Christian couple who took us to a pastor who was of African descent. I would later discover that this pastor had the gift of prophecy.

The pastor prophesied over the individuals who went with us to this small building, but it was what he prophesied over me that was stuck with me forever. He stated, "Whoa! You are going to have a big testimony and bring many people to God with it!". I was skeptical and just shrugged it off, not truly knowing what would happen later on in my life. Fast forward about 2 years after I finished my first battle with cancer, I relapsed around the same spot as previously mentioned. It extremely devastated me about this because of having more scheduled chemo and needing to amputate my right leg. I would take a lot of time being on my own around this time in hopes of mentally preparing myself. One day, I parked at a lake and began praying to God from my heart. I did not know what it truly meant to pray, so I just began speaking to him from what was in my mind and heart. I said, "God if you are truly genuine, show me & if you care about me, show me".

About 15 minutes later, I went to cancel a gym membership at LA Fitness, where I saw one of my friends working. I explained to him why I was canceling my membership and he questioned why I wanted to cancel. He then said, "Man! You should go to my church. I have seen many miracles there and people be healed". I had nothing to lose, so I began going. He began showing me the verses in the book of Acts about baptism and being filled with the Holy Ghost. He told me about the whole speaking in tongues, which I found weird, but he directed me to biblical evidence. The next thing I knew, I was at his church when they asked who wanted to surrender their life to Christ and be baptized. I approached the pulpit when a pastor placed his hand over my head. He began praying for me and I began speaking in tongues the same day they baptized me. This landed the mark of my being a born-again experience, not knowing that I was now in the spiritual war.

Even after this experience, I began getting attacked and drawn away from God. I would also like to mention that even before I was baptized, demons spiritually attacked me, and even heard a few of them audibly. I heard one laughing in a child's voice outside my window at 3 am, one laughing as it touched me sexually, and one telling me it was going to take me to hell. There are a few more attacks I have experienced, but those are the ones that stand out the most. Now, back to where I left off about getting drawn away from God. I had a relationship with a girl who eventually cheated on me and broke my heart into pieces. We were together for about one year and it ended tragically. As I was trying to cope with the emptiness, I began to drink and smoke. I then began asking God to help me and bring me close to him again while I was in tears. I truly meant this and began experiencing the mercy of God, not really knowing what that really was.

I began going to church again with my friend and his mom where I was baptized in the Pentecostal church. This is when my knowledge of the Bible began growing immensely. I went through foundation courses and learned so much by reading God's word. My friend's mom eventually gave me Elizabeth Das's book "I did it His Way" telling me it was an influential book about her walk with God. When I finished the book, I noticed that her email was on it. I reached out to Elizabeth and my friend's mom told her about me as well. I began speaking to her on the phone and eventually meeting her in person. Since I met her, I noticed that she really loves and applies God's word to her life. She has laid hands on the sick and prays for many people in her own time. I consider her my spiritual mentor, as she has taught me so much about God and his word, which I am extremely grateful for. I would say we have even become friends and continue to check on each other to this day.

In January 2017, I was under an apartment lease that belonged to the university I was attending. I was actually trying to get someone to take over my lease because of financial issues. I was not working and did not have money to continue paying rent for the apartment. Unfortunately, I could not find someone to take over my lease, which would leave me responsible for continuing to pay the rent. I called Elizabeth Das as I do often for prayer about this issue of breaking the contract clean. That same January, I had a CT scan on my chest which revealed I had a spot on the right lower lobe of my lung. I had to go through surgery to remove the spot that was shown on the scan, which turned out to be malignant. Although this sucked, I could get off the contract lease for the apartment that same month because of this. They say God works in mysterious ways, so I trusted him with what was going on. During this time, I was doing my pre-req classes, hoping to finish and get accepted into nursing school. Elizabeth would pray for me to get a good job and get into nursing school according to God's will for my life.

About three months later, I was scheduled to have another CT scan of my chest to see if I was doing okay. However, the scan showed another spot on my lung, close to the same one that was there in January 2017.

The oncologist said that he believes this is cancer coming back again and we need to get it removed through surgery. I couldn't believe this was going on. I thought that this was it for me. I told Elizabeth about it and so many other people began praying for me at this time. Although this was going on, I still had a little faith that everything was going to be fine and that God would take care of me. I recall driving one day at night and asking God, "If you get me out of this mess, I promise to share what you have done for me with others".

A few weeks later, I went to get surgery, and they removed a larger diameter of the right lower lobe of my lung. Elizabeth and her friend even came to the hospital to lay hands on me and pray that God would bring healing to me. About two weeks later after the surgery, I went back to the hospital to get my results. Not to mention I was still looking for a job at a hospital to better my chances of getting into nursing school during this time. As I approached the check-in desk that same day to get my results for the surgery, I asked if they were hiring. One manager was there at the front as I was checking in and gave me her information to let her know when I submit my application online. Next thing you know; I was waiting in a room for the oncologist to show up with my results. I was extremely nervous and fearful of what he would tell me.

The oncologist came into the room and the first thing he said was, "Has anybody told you your results yet?". I told him no and wanted him to just lay my options down on the table on what I must do next. He then told me, "So your results showed it was just calcium build-up, it's not cancer." I was completely in shock, knowing that it was God who did this for me. I went to my car and began crying tears of joy! I called Elizabeth and told her the good news. We both celebrated together. A few days later, I was interviewed for the job at the hospital and just a week later, they offered me the job. A few weeks after I received the job, I got accepted into nursing school. Glory to God for putting all of this together, as it still brings joy to me talking about it.

At this moment, I am in my last semester of nursing school and graduating in May 2019. I have experienced so much and am grateful for all the doors that God has opened and closed for me. I have even found myself in a relationship with another and she has been amazing to me being there since cancer metastasized to my lung in January 2017 to the present moment today. Elizabeth has taught me so much and has prayed for me plenty of times, which shows me the power of prayer and the laying of hands on the sick. Reader, I am not in any way more special than you. God loves you equally and Jesus Christ has died for your sins and mine. If you seek him with all your heart, you will find him.

"For I know the thoughts that I think toward you, saith the Lord, thoughts of peace, and not of evil, to give you an expected end. Then shall ye call upon me, and ye shall go and pray unto me, and I will hearken unto you. And ye shall seek me, and find me, when ye shall search for me with all your heart" Jeremiah 29:11-13 KJV.

Madalyn Ascencio
El Monte, California, U.S.A.

I used to believe that a man would complete me. When I fell in Love with Jesus I found that it is Him and Him alone who completes me. I was created to worship and adore Him! My name is Madalyn Ascencio and this is my testimony.

In March 2005 I began to suffer from anxiety and panic attacks for 3 years. I went to the hospital on several occasions and all they offered was antidepressants and Valium but I refused to be dependent on medication to feel normal. I prayed for God to help me. One Saturday morning in mid October 2008, I had a very bad panic attack so I called Sister Elizabeth. She asked me what was happening and she prayed for me. Once I felt better she gave me some scriptures to read. I prayed and asked God to give me wisdom and understanding. As I read the scriptures,

*John 3:5-7: Jesus answered, Verily, verily, I say unto thee, **except a man be born of water and of the Spirit, he cannot enter into the***

kingdom of God. *That which is born of the flesh is flesh; and that which is born of the Spirit is spirit. Marvel not that I said unto thee, Ye must be born again.*

John 8:32: And ye shall know the truth, and the truth shall make you free.

John 10:10: The thief cometh not, but for to steal, and to kill, and to destroy: I am come that they might have life, and that they might have it more abundant

I knew that God was speaking to me. The more I prayed and spoke with Sister Elizabeth, I knew I needed to be re-baptized. I had been praying so much that God would draw me closer. I attended a Christian non-denominational church from 2001 through 2008 and in April 2007 I was baptized. Sister Elizabeth asked me what I felt when I got baptized and I told her "I felt good". Her response was "that's it"? She asked if I was baptized in Jesus Name and I told her I was baptized in the name of the Father, the Son and the Holy Spirit. She told me to read and study.

*Acts 2:38: Then Peter said unto them, Repent, and be baptized every one of you in the **name of Jesus Christ for the remission of sins**, and ye shall receive the gift of the Holy Ghost.*

*Acts 8:12-17: But when they believed Philip preaching the things concerning the kingdom of God, and the name of Jesus Christ, they were baptized, both men and women. Then Simon himself believed also: and when he was baptized, he continued with Philip, and wondered, beholding the miracles and signs which were done. Now when the apostles which were at Jerusalem heard that Samaria had received the word of God, they sent unto them Peter and John: Who, when they were come down, prayed for them, that they might receive the Holy Ghost: (For as yet he was fallen upon none of them: only they were **baptized in the name of the Lord Jesus.**) Then laid they their hands on them, and they received the Holy Ghost.*

*Acts 10:43-48: To him give all the prophets witness, that through his name whosoever believeth in him shall receive remission of sins. While Peter yet spake these words, the Holy Ghost fell on all them which heard the word. And they of the circumcision which believed were astonished, as many as came with Peter, because that on the Gentiles also was poured out the gift of the Holy Ghost. For they heard them speak with tongues, and magnify God. Then answered Peter, Can any man forbid water, that these should not be baptized, which have received the Holy Ghost as well as we? And he **commanded them to be baptized in the name of the Lord.***

*Acts 19:1-6: And it came to pass, that, while Apollos was at Corinth, Paul having passed through the upper coasts came to Ephesus: and finding certain disciples, He said unto them, Have ye received the Holy Ghost since ye believed? And they said unto him, We have not so much as heard whether there be any Holy Ghost. And he said unto them, Unto what then were ye baptized? And they said, Unto John's baptism. Then said Paul, John verily baptized with the baptism of repentance, saying unto the people, that they should believe on him which should come after him, that is, on Christ Jesus. When they heard this, **they were baptized in the name of the Lord Jesus**. And when Paul had laid his hands upon them, the Holy Ghost came on them; and they spake with tongues, and prophesied.*

*Acts 22:16 And now why tarriest thou? arise, and be **baptized, and wash away thy sins, calling on the name of the Lord.***

The Lord revealed to me that the Holy Ghost was also available for me and if I were to be **baptized in the Name of Jesus** I would be healed and delivered from this terrible suffering. On the days that it was real bad I would call Sister Elizabeth and she prayed over me. I realized I was being attacked by the enemy, after all, his mission is to steal, kill and destroy as it states in John 10:10. Many years ago I read Ephesians 6:10-18 and realized I needed to wear the Whole Armor of God daily. Every time I began to feel anxiety overtake me I began to fight and not fear. On November 2, 2008 I was baptized in Jesus Name at Life Church,

Pasadena, CA. I felt the most amazing Peace that I have never known before and that was before I even got in the water to be baptized. When I came up out of the water, I felt as light as a feather as if I were walking on clouds and could not stop smiling. I felt God's Presence, Peace and Love like never before. On November 16, 2008 I received the gift of the Holy Ghost by evidence of speaking in other tongues. The void I always felt since I was a child was now filled. I knew God loved me and had a great purpose for my life and the more I seek him and pray the more he reveals Himself to me. God has shown me that I am to share my Faith, give Hope, and Love. Since my new apostolic birth and deliverance from anxiety, Jesus has brought many people into my life that also suffer from anxiety. I now have a ministry in my testimony to share with them.

I am so very grateful to Jesus for Sister Elizabeth Das. It was through her prayers and teaching that I am now working for Jesus too. She also led my mother, daughter, aunt and some friends to the Lord through her prayers and ministry. I was created to give Jesus all the Glory! Blessed be His Holy Name.

Martin Razo
Santa Ana, California, U.S.A.

As a kid I lived in sorrow. Although people surrounded me, I had the feeling of deep loneliness. My name is Martin Razo and this was my childhood growing up. In high school everyone knew who I was, even if they were not in the circle of what I considered the "cool people." I had a couple of girlfriends, did drugs and lived life like this was something normal because almost everyone else did it. Friday and Saturday night I got high with my friends and went to clubs to pick up girls. My father was always on my back watching what I did and where.

Family friend sister Elizabeth was sharing her testimony with me. It was not boring, as a matter of fact; it was actually very interesting what she was saying. I used to think that she actually believed what she was saying. Then suddenly everything went wrong at home. It seemed as though the Lord was warning me and calling me through fear. I had three very frightening experiences that made me believe this. First, I was caught with drugs and ran away from home but not for long. My aunt made me call my mother and after hearing that my mom had diabetes, I returned home. Second, I was coming from a night club at 2:00 o'clock in the morning and got into an auto accident where the car blew up and went into the air. I was attending Bible study with Sister Das during that time. Three, I asked a friend for a ride and as we began talking, he told me that he had sold his soul to the devil and how he had power to turn lights on and off. Using the streetlights, he demonstrated it to me by blinking his eyes to turn them on and off. I saw his face as though it was transforming into a demon. I jumped out of the car and ran home as fast as I could. Hours later I got to thinking about what Sister Elizabeth said and thought it must be real too. Sister Das gave me a Bible study over the phone on the baptism in the Name of Jesus as spoken in the Book of Acts and the early church. She did not know about my suicidal tendency at the time but something told her that I needed to hear it right away because she may not see me again. I got baptized while I was attending a church that believed that God is a holy trinity of three persons. I was making the transition from that church to the doctrine of the apostles. God is One! God is Spirit, Jesus was God come in the flesh to dwell among men and the Holy Ghost is God in us. This was and is the doctrine of the Apostles. I had only accepted what I was taught as being truth. I did not know the origin of when and where this belief came from.

A week later, Sister Elizabeth asked me to go to my uncle's house for a Bible study. Brother James Min who has the gift of healing and deliverance came with her. There were miracles that night and after the Bible study, they asked us if we wanted to receive the Holy Spirit. Most of us said yes. I was still thinking this is crazy and not possible but I stepped forward anyway.

As Brother James and Sister Elizabeth prayed for me, a power came over me. I didn't know how to respond to this powerful feeling of joy. First I suppressed the feeling of this power. Then a second time, it came more powerful than the first time, it got stronger as I tried to suppress it again.

The third time I could not suppress the Spirit and I started to speak in another tongue or language I didn't know. I thought that speaking in tongues was a lie, so when the joy of the Holy Spirit first came over me; I was trying to speak, but tried to stop it, because I was scared. Jesus healed me from all depression and suicidal thoughts that day.

I am 28 years old now and the Lord has truly changed my life for the better. I have completed Bible School and the Lord blessed me with a beautiful wife. We have a youth Ministry at our church and I am also pursuing a ministry as a Servant of God. Sister Das never gave up on the Razo Family or me. Because of her many prayers and sharing her testimonies of the power of God, good has come to the whole Razo Family. Many of our relatives and neighbors have also turned to the Lord Jesus Christ. Now I have a testimony. Let me say that you must never ever give up praying for loved ones and people in general. You may never know what God is doing and how he strategizes in order to accomplish it His Way!!

Tammy Alford
Mount. Herman, Louisiana, U.S.A.

I have basically been in church all of my life. My burden is for the people that are hurting and want to reach them with the Word of Truth to let them know that Jesus is their Hope. When the Lord gave me this burden, I wrote "The People" on a prayer cloth and shared it with my church. We began praying and interceding, and as a result, everyone received a prayer cloth to take home to pray over it.

 It was through our former pastor and his family (who have now been called to India as Missionaries) that I first met Sis. Elizabeth Das. Our Country Church in Franklinton, Louisiana, welcomed her as she shared her powerful testimony. Everyone was blessed. A few months later, Sis Elizabeth and I became Prayer Partners. A Radiant Lady who not only loves to pray but lives it! Amazingly true she lives, "In Season and Out of Season." Our Prayer time was in the early morning by telephone, Texas connecting with Louisiana. We had the blessings of the Lord. He gave the increase and soon we had a prayer group from different states.

Through a conference shared-line we began praying and fasting then praise reports started coming in. Our God is So Amazing! Sister Elizabeth is that Radiant Woman who has such a burning desire to see souls saved. Her burning Flame has sparked and ignited many others to Pray and has Vision. There is no sickness, pain, or devil in hell that will stop her. For many years now she has been reaching and praying for the lost and dying; only eternity will tell. I thank God for her bulldog determination and her love for "The People." I've seen God do awesome works, miracles and answer prayers through her. My friends here and people I'm acquainted with all can testify that when we call Sis. Elizabeth, the prayer of faith is prayed. Things Happen! For instance, a lady who attends our church from time to time was due for a major surgery. Although she lived out of town I told her I would call Sister Elizabeth and we would pray for her illness over the phone. We prayed and her pain was gone. Sister Elizabeth told her, "No need for surgery you are healed." She remained scheduled for surgery until the hospital called to cancel her surgery and she went forth and rescheduled it. The hospital did not perform anymore pre-op testing and went ahead with the surgery. After the surgery she was informed that they found nothing wrong with her, not even a trace of the serious disease.

Another miracle was regarding my friend who has a small boy. He was sick with fever and had fallen asleep. We called Sis. Elizabeth and prayed on the speaker phone. The young boy suddenly woke, got up running around normally and was healed. Many times we have prayed over homes with demonic spirits and we could actually feel that something had happened. We would rejoice in the report of them telling us they felt sudden peace or they could get a good night's sleep without being tormented.

I know my faith has increased since becoming a part of this prayer group. Sister Elizabeth has been a teacher to me in so many ways. She has given me spiritual guidance through the Word of God. Her life is that beautiful example, displaying the metaphors in the Bible where it speaks about the "light upon the hill which cannot be hid" and also 'The tree planted by the rivers of water." Her roots are deeply rooted in Jesus and she is able to supply others with the strength and wisdom they need. Through the dark trials I've walked, I know Sis. Elizabeth has prayed me through and I am thankful for her ministry. She is truly that dazzling Jewel chosen in Christ being used mightily for His Kingdom. Early every morning she brings those empty vessels before Jesus and He fills them full all over again. My thanks to Sister Elizabeth for truly, yet purely giving herself to Jesus and His Kingdom. To God Be the Glory!

Rhonda Callahan
Fort Worth, Texas
May 20, 2011

Sometime in 2007 I was driving through the city of Dallas along an over pass, I noticed a couple of homeless men sleeping under a bridge. I was

Elizabeth Das

moved with compassion and said to the Lord "Lord if you were on this earth today, you would touch those men and heal their minds and make them whole! They would become productive men of the community living normal lives".... Immediately Jesus spoke to my heart and said "You are my hands and you are my feet." I knew at that moment what God was speaking to me. I began to cry and praise Him. I possessed the power to touch those men and make them whole. Not of my own power, but of His power.

According to Acts 1:8 "But ye shall receive power, after that the Holy Ghost is come upon you: and ye shall be witnesses unto me both in Jerusalem, and in all Judaea, and in Samaria, and unto the uttermost part of the earth.

Furthermore, Ephesians 1:13-14 Tells us;

"In whom ye also trusted, after that ye heard the word of truth, the gospel of your salvation: in whom also after that ye believed, ye were sealed with that holy Spirit of promise, which is the earnest of our inheritance until the redemption of the purchased possession, unto the praise of his glory."

I had received the power and been sealed in 1986 when God gloriously baptized me with the Holy Ghost. So many times we have the mindset that if God was here today, Miracles would happen among us. We must understand that when He fills you with His Holy Spirit. He has given you power to do miracles. We become His hands and feet, we are called to preach this wonderful message to all who are in need.

Luke 4:18

"The Spirit of the Lord is upon me, because he hath anointed me to preach the gospel to the poor; he hath sent me to heal the brokenhearted, to preach deliverance to the captives, and recovering of sight to the blind, to set at liberty them that are bruised, to preach the acceptable year of the Lord".

Even though I had been filled with the Holy Ghost since 1986, I had been dealt some hard blows over the last few years. I attended church faithfully; I was a Sunday school teacher and just completed 4 years of Bible College. Volunteered to do whatever was asked of me at church.

Yet, I had become extremely oppressed. I still believed God was able to do all that He had promised, but I was a broken vessel. There was once a time I labored before the Lord in prayer and intercession, read my Bible every day, witnessed every chance I got, but now found myself not praying much at all. Discouraged and depressed, I was over whelmed with constant mental torment. My daughter had recently left her husband and filed for a divorce. My grandson was 4 yrs old at the time, and I saw the pain he was suffering from a broken home. I grew more tormented by thoughts of the life he would live being raised in a broken home. I worried about the possibility of being abused by a step parent, who had no love for him, or the possibility growing up not feeling loved by his father or mother because of this divorce. My mind raced with awful thoughts and I cried daily. I express these thoughts to a few close friends. They always responded the same way... Trust God! I knew God was able, but I had lost faith in myself. When I did pray, I found myself begging, weeping, and wishing for God to keep him safe. I knew He could, but would He for me?

I battled over eating, and continually needed to stuff myself. My flesh had become the ruler of my life. I no longer walked in the spirit but, walked more in the flesh and fulfilling the lust of the flesh continually or at least that's how I felt.

March 27, 2011 we had a Ladies Fellowship lunch after church. I was asked to speak. Remember I was still working in the church as normal, but I was broken and few if any understood the depth of my brokenness. After the luncheon Sister Elizabeth Das walked up to me with a sweet smile and gave me her phone number. She said "call me if you ever need a place to go after church, you can stay at my house." The reason she told me I could stay with her is because it is a 65-mile drive to church for me one way and it is very hard to go home and return again for the evening service so I just tried to hang around until the evening service instead of driving back home between services.

About two weeks had past and I felt as though I was more depressed. One morning on my way to work I dug through my purse and found Sister Elizabeth's number. I called her and asked her to please pray for me.

Expecting her to say ok and end the phone call. But to my surprise, she said I will pray for you now. I pulled my car over to the side of the road and she prayed for me.

The following week after church I went home with her. After talking a while, she asked to pray for me. She laid her hands upon my head and began to pray. With power and authority in her voice, she prayed for God to deliver me. She rebuked the darkness that surrounded me; over eating, mental torment, depression and oppression.

I know that day God used those hands to deliver me from the awful oppression I suffered. The moment Sister Elizabeth yielded to God, He set me free!

Mark 16:17-18 tells us "And these signs shall follow them that believe; In my name shall they cast out devils; they shall speak with new tongues; They shall take up serpents; and if they drink any deadly thing, it shall not hurt them; they shall lay hands on the sick, and they shall recover".

Isaiah 61:1 "The Spirit of the Lord GOD is upon me; because the LORD hath anointed me to preach good tidings unto the meek; he hath sent me to bind up the brokenhearted, to proclaim liberty to the captives, and the opening of the prison to them that are bound;".

Jesus needs us to be His hands and feet. Sis. Elizabeth is a true servant of God. Being filled with His power and being obedient to His voice.

I'm so thankful that there are women like Sis. Elizabeth walking among us, who still believe in the delivering power of Jesus' precious blood, who have been anointed by His Spirit and fulfilling that wonderful calling He has called her to do. That day God turned my pain into beauty and removed the spirit of heaviness replacing it with the oil of joy.

Isaiah 61:3 "To appoint unto them that mourn in Zion, to give unto them beauty for ashes, the oil of joy for mourning, the garment of praise for the spirit of heaviness; that they might be called trees of righteousness, the planting of the LORD, that he might be glorified".

I challenge you today; seek God with your whole heart that ye may walk in the fullness of His power. He needs you to share Jesus with others and be His hands and feet. Amen!

Vicky Franzen Josephine
Texas

My name is Vicki Franzen, I attended the Catholic Church most of my adult life; however, I always felt as though something was missing. A few years ago, I began listening to a Radio program that taught about the End Time. Many questions that I had all my life were answered. This led me to an apostolic church to continue my search for truth. There, I was baptized in the name of Jesus and received the baptism of the Holy Ghost, with the evidence of speaking in tongues, as described in the book of Acts.

The next four years, it seemed that the ability to speak in tongues was not available to me any longer; even though I attended church regularly, prayed, studied, and was involved in different ministries. I felt very "dry" and void of the Holy Spirit. Another member of my church told me when Sister Liz had laid hands on her and prayed, that "something" came out of her; making her feel completely free from oppression, depression, and etc.

Several ladies from our church were meeting for lunch, which gave me the opportunity to meet Sister Elizabeth. A conversation began about demons and the spiritual world. I had always been very curious about this subject, but had never heard a teaching on it. We exchanged phone numbers and began a Bible study in her home. I questioned how a person who had been baptized in Jesus' name and baptized with the Holy Ghost could have a demon. She told me that you have to live a righteous holy life by praying, fasting, reading the word of God, and staying full of the Holy Ghost by speaking in tongues every day. At that time, I shared my experience of feeling dry and not being able to speak in tongues. She laid hands on me and prayed. I felt good, but very tired. Liz explained that when an evil spirit comes out of the body, it leaves you feeling tired and drained. She continued praying over me and I began speaking in tongues. I was so excited and full of joy. Being able to speak in tongues, let me know that I still had the Holy Ghost.

Liz and I became good friends, praying together. Sister Elizabeth has such a sweet and gentle spirit about her, but when she prays, God anoints her with godly boldness to heal the sick and to cast out demons. She prays with authority and nearly always sees the answer immediately. God has given her a talent for teaching scripture that makes the meaning, very clear to me.

I was telling Liz about my friend Valerie's daughter, Mary. She was diagnosed with ADD and COPD. She also had ruptured discs that they were trying to treat without surgery. She was constantly in the hospital with various physical issues. She was on a lot of different medications without any good results. Mary was so disabled that she could not work; and had four children to care for without any support from her ex-husband.

Sister Liz began to tell me that some of those things are demons and can be cast out in the name of Jesus. I had some doubts about that simply because of not ever hearing that, particular illness referred to as being caused by demons. When my friend, her Mother-in-law, and I sat down for coffee recently, they began to tell me how viscously Mary spoke to them. She screamed, yelled, and cursed at them. They knew she had experienced a great deal of pain with her back issues and severe headaches which the medications did not seem to relieve; however, this was different. They spoke of how hateful her eyes were at times and how much it scared them.

A few days later, my friend called to say she could not take it anymore! The descriptions of how her daughter was acting began to confirm the things that Sis. Liz was telling me about Demons. Everything she told me, God confirmed through others. Mary's condition was getting worse and she began to talk about ending her life. We began to pray in agreement for the casting out of demons in Mary and her home. God woke Sister Liz up two nights in a row to intercede for Mary. Liz specifically asked God to show Mary what was going on there.

When Mary was praying in the night she had a vision that her husband (who left her and was living with another woman) was in her house. She thought the vision was God's answer to her prayer that he would be coming back home to them for Christmas. Sister Liz told me that she suspected witch craft was being used against Mary. Probably by her ex-husband or the woman he was living with. I really didn't understand how she could know that. I did not share any of the things Liz told me with anyone. Within a couple of days, Valerie told me that her daughter, Mary was receiving strange ugly text messages from the woman that lives with her ex-husband. Mary knew the language was definitely used for witch craft. This was a confirmation of what Sister Liz had told me.

Over the past couple of months of knowing about Mary's condition, we had tried to go and pray for her. It just never worked out. Sister Liz said, "even though we cannot make it to her house, God will go and take care of the situation."

And when Jesus was entered into Capernaum, there came unto him a centurion, beseeching him, And saying, Lord, my servant lieth at home sick of the palsy, grievously tormented. And Jesus saith unto him, I will come and heal him. The centurion answered and said, Lord, I am not worthy that thou shouldest come under my roof: but speak the word only, and my servant shall be healed. For I am a man under authority, having soldiers under me: and I say to this man, Go, and he goeth; and to another, Come, and he cometh; and to my servant, Do this, and he doeth it. When Jesus heard it, he marvelled, and said to them that followed, Verily I say unto you, I have not found so great faith, no, not in Israel. (Mathew 8: 5-10)

Within two days of us praying to cast out demons from Mary and her home, she reported to her mother, that she was sleeping better and had no more dreams. This is one of many things Sis. Liz told me, that when you have many dreams and night mares, it can be an indication of evil spirits in your house. The following day a coworker of Valerie's told her about a dream that she had the night before. A flat black snake was crawling away from Mary's house. That day Mary called her mother to say she felt so happy and joyful. She was out shopping with her 15 month old twins; which she had not done in quite some time. This was another confirmation that ADD, ADHD, Bipolar, and Schizophrenia are attacks of the enemy. We have power over scorpions and serpents (These are all evil spirits that are mentioned in the Bible.) which we can cast out only, in the name of Jesus.

Behold, I give unto you power to tread on serpents and scorpions, and over all the power of the enemy: and nothing shall by any means hurt you. Luke 10:19

Sister Liz also told me that we must anoint our family, our homes, and ourselves with blessed olive oil daily from attacks of the enemy. We should also let the word of God permeate our home.

This experience has helped me to see some situations that are definitely controlled by demons as spoken of in the Bible.

For we wrestle not against flesh and blood, but against principalities, against powers, against the rulers of the darkness of this world, against spiritual wickedness in high places. (Ephesians 6:12)

I can only speak for myself. I grew up believing that miracles, speaking in tongues, healing the sick, and casting out demons were only for the Bible times, when Jesus and His Apostles were on the earth. I never thought much about demon possession in our present day. I now know and understand; we are still in Bible times! His Word has always been for the present. The "present" was yesterday, the "present" is now, and the "present" will be for tomorrow!

Jesus Christ the same yesterday, and today, and forever. (Hebrew 13:8)

Satan has managed to deceive and lead us away from the power God gave His Church. God's Church is those that repent, are baptized in the name of Jesus, and receive the gift of the Holy Ghost, with the evidence of speaking in tongues. They will then receive power from upon high.

But ye shall receive power, after that the Holy Ghost is come upon you: and ye shall be witnesses unto me both in Jerusalem, and in all Judaea, and in Samaria, and unto the uttermost part of the earth. (Acts 1:8)

And my speech and my preaching was not with enticing words of man's wisdom, but in demonstration of the Spirit and of power (1 Corinthians 2:4)

For our gospel came not unto you in word only, but also in power, and in the Holy Ghost, and in much assurance; as ye know what manner of men we were among you for your sake. (1 Thessalonians 1:5)

God's Word is for us NOW!

Section II

I never thought about putting this second part in my book. However, I took the time and added this part because so many people requested the information. Ever since I began giving Bible studies to different nationalities, we came across changes in the modern Bibles. I began to dig deep into history and found some very shocking information. Having this information, I believe it is my responsibility to let my fellow brothers and sisters know this truth and to stop the enemy in his tracks so he will no longer mislead people.

A.
Languages God Used

O ver the centuries, the Bible has taken many different modes and more noticeably, different languages. Throughout history we see four main languages that the Bible has been translated into: first, Hebrew, then Greek, followed by Latin, and finally English. The subsequent paragraphs briefly show these different stages.

From around 2000 B.C., the time of Abraham to approximately 70 A.D., the time of the destruction of the second temple in Jerusalem, God chose to speak to His people through the Semitic languages, mostly Hebrew. It was through this language that his chosen people were shown the way, and also that they were indeed in need of a Savior to correct them when they sinned.

As the world progressed, a super power arose; this power's main communication was through the Greek language. Greek was a prominent language for three centuries, and was a logical choice by God. It was through Greek that God chose to communicate the New Testament; and as proven by history, it spread like wildfire. Realizing the eminent threat that would be a text written in the language of the masses, Satan set out to destroy the Bible's credibility. This "fake" Bible was written in Greek but originated in Alexandria Egypt; the Old Testament referred to as the

"Septuagint" and the New Testament was called the "Alexandrian Text". The information was perverted by man's ideas and deleted many of God's words. It is also apparent that today this Apocrypha (Greek meaning 'Hidden', were never considered as the word of God) has seeped into our modern Bible.

By 120 AD Latin had become a common language, and the Bible was translated again in the 1500s. Because Latin was such a widely spoken language at the time, the Bible was easily read throughout Europe. Latin, at the time was considered an "international" language. This allowed the Bible to travel through the countries and be further translated into regional dialects. This early version was called the Vulgate, meaning "common Bible". The Devil responded to this threat by creating a sister book in Rome. The Roman's claimed that their Bible, which was filled with the "thrown out books" of the Apocrypha and texts that were meant to resemble the real Bible, was in fact the true Bible. At this point we have two Bibles which were dramatically different from each other; in order to protect his fake Bible the Devil had to set out and destroy the true texts. The Roman Catholics sent mercenaries to annihilate and martyr those who were in possession of the true Latin Vulgate. The mercenaries were successful for the most part, but in the end were unable to completely eradicate it, and God's word was preserved.

Between the years of 600-700 AD, a new world language developed, English. God began laying the ground work which then triggered a massive missionary movement. First, William Tyndale in the 1500s, began to translate the original Hebrew and Greek texts into the new language. Many after him attempted to do the same, trying their best to match the previous Hebrew and Greek texts. Among these people were King James VI who, in 1604 commissioned a council to produce the most accurate English version of the texts. By 1611 an authorized version was in circulation, commonly known as the King James Bible. Missionaries began translating from this Bible all around the world.

Satan's continous attack on the Word of God:

Now we are facing another attack of the devil. The Bible published in 2011 claiming it is the 1611 KJV, inserted the Apocrypha, which was never considered the Word of God. The Apocrypha was removed from the KJV by the Authorized Scholars knowing the fact it was not the word of God.

Satan never gives up!

B.
How God Preserved His Word?

God places the highest importance upon His written word, which is abundantly clear.

The words of the LORD are pure words: as silver tried in a furnace of earth, purified seven times. Thou shalt keep them, O LORD, thou shalt preserve them from this generation forever (Pslams 12:6-7)

The Word of God is above all names:

*"I will worship toward thy holy temple, and praise thy name for thy lovingkindness and for thy truth: <u>**for thou hast magnified thy word above all thy name**</u>." (Psalms 138:2)*

The Lord also warned us of His view of His word. He gave serious warnings to those who would corrupt the Scriptures. God warned against adding to His word:

<u>***Every word of God is pure***</u>*: he is a shield unto them that put their trust in him. Add thou not unto his words, lest he reprove thee, and thou be found a liar. (Proverb 30:5-6)*

God has preserved His Words to all generations, without fail!

Many devout men were heroically trying to hold back the rising tide of apostasy and unbelief; due in part, to the diluting of the authority of the Word of God. During the Dark Ages, the Catholic Church controlled the people by having the Bible written in Latin only. The common people could not read or speak Latin.

By 400 AD, the Bible was translated into 500 languages from the original manuscripts that were true. In order to control people, the Catholic Church made a harsh law that the Bible could only be written and read in the Latin language. This Latin version was not translated from the original manuscripts.

John Wycliffe:

John Wycliffe was well known as a pastor, a scholar, an Oxford professor, and a theologian. In 1371 J.W. started hand writing the manuscripts into English, with the help of many faithful scribes and followers. Wycliffe's first hand written English language Bible manuscript was translated from the Latin Vulgate. This would help put a stop to the false teachings of the Roman Catholic Church. It would take 10 months and cost forty pounds to write and distribute just one copy of the Bible. God's hand was on Wycliffe. The Roman Catholic Church raged in anger against Mr. Wycliffe. His many substantial friends helped him from being harmed. Although the Catholic Church did everything in its power to collect and burn every copy, that did not stop Wycliffe. He never gave up because he knew his work was not in vain. The Catholic Church was unsuccessful with obtaining all the copies. One hundred seventy copies remained. To God Be the Glory!

The Roman Catholic Church continued in their anger. Forty-four years after the death of John Wycliffe, the Pope ordered his bones to be dug up, crushed, and thrown into the river. Around one hundred years following the death of J. Wycliffe, Europe began learning Greek.

John Hus:

One of John Wycliffe's followers, John Hus, continued the work that Wycliffe had started; he too opposed false teachings. The Catholic Church was determined to stop any changes other then their own, by threatening execution for anyone who read a non-Latin Bible. Wycliffe's idea, that the Bible should be translated into ones' own language would avail. John Hus was burned at the stake in 1415 along with Mr. Wycliffe's manuscript that was used to ignite the fire. His last words were, "In 100 years, God will raise up a man whose calls for reform cannot be suppressed!". In 1517, his prophecy came true, when Martin Luther posted his famous Thesis of Contention on the Catholic Church at Wittenberg. In the same year Fox's book of Martyrs, records that the Roman Catholic Church burnt 7 people at the stake for the crime of "teaching their children to pray, The Lords prayer in English instead of Latin."

Johannes Guttenberg:

The first book to be printed in the printing press was the Latin Language Bible and was invented by Johannes Guttenberg in 1440.

This invention allowed a large number of books to be printed in a very short period of time. This would prove to be a vital instrument in pushing the Protestant Reformation forward.

Dr. Thomas Linacre:

Dr. Thomas Linacre, an Oxford professor, decided to learn Greek in the 1490's. He read and finished the Bible in the original Greek language. After finishing his studies he stated "Either this is not the Gospel or we are not Christian".

The Roman Catholic Latin Vulgate versions had become so corrupted that the truth was hid. The Catholic Church continued trying to enforce their strict harsh law of demanding that people read the Bible in the Latin language only.

John Colet:

In 1496, John Colet another Oxford professor started to translate the Bible from Greek to English for his students and later for the public at St. Paul's Cathedral in London. Within six months, revival broke out and over 40,000 people attended his service. He encouraged people to fight for Christ and not to be involved in religious wars. Having many friends in high places, he escaped execution.

Desiderius Erasmus, 1466-1536:

Mr. Desiderius Erasmus, a great scholar observed the events of Mr. Colet and Mr. Linacre. He was impressed to convert the Latin Vulgate back to the truth. It was accomplished with the help of Mr. J. Froben, who printed and published the manuscript in 1516.

Mr. Erasmus wanted everyone to know how corrupted the Latin Vulgate had become. He encouraged them to turn their focus on the truth. He stressed the fact that by using the original manuscripts, which were in Greek and Hebrew, it would keep one on the right path of continuing in faithfulness and freedom.

One of the most famous and amusing quotes from the noted scholar and translator Erasmus was,

"When I get a little money I buy books; and if any is left I buy food and clothes".

The Catholic Church continued to attack anyone who was found participating in any translation of the Bible other than Latin.

William Tyndale (1494-1536):

Mr. William Tyndale was born in 1494 and died at the age of 42. Mr. Tyndale was not only the captain of the army of reformers, he was also known as their spiritual leader. He was a great man of integrity and respect. Mr. Tyndale attended Oxford University where he studied and grew up. After receiving his master degree at the age of twenty-one, he left for London.

He was gifted in speaking many languages: Hebrew, Greek, Spanish, German, Latin, French, Italian and English. One of Mr. Tyndale's associates said that when anyone heard him speak one of these languages, they would think he was speaking in his native tongue. He used these languages to bless others. He translated the Greek New Testament into English. Amazingly, he was the first man to print the Bible in English. Without a doubt, this gift enabled his escapes to be successful from the authorities, during his years of exile from England. Eventually Mr. Tyndale was caught and arrested for the crime of heresy and treason. In October of 1536, after an unfair trial and five hundred days in a prison with miserable conditions, Mr. Tyndale was burned at the stake. It is recorded that the Tyndale House Publishers is a modern company named after this amazing hero.

Martin Luther:

The Roman Catholic Church had ruled for too long and Martin Luther had no tolerance for the corruption within the church. He was fed up with the false teachings that were forced on the people. On Halloween of 1517, he had no second thoughts, when he posted his 95 Thesis of Contention on the church of Wittenberg. The Diet of Worms council formed by the church, planned to martyr Martin Luther. The Catholic Church feared the eventual loss of power and income. No longer would they be able to sell indulgences for sins or the release of loved ones from "purgatory", which is a doctrine made up by the Catholic Church.

Martin Luther had a head start on Tyndale and in September of 1522, he published his first translation of the Greek-Latin New Testament of Erasmus into German. Tyndale wanted to use the same original text. He began the process and was terrorized by the authorities. He left England in 1525 for Germany where he worked by Martin Luther's side. By the end of the year the New Testament was translated into English language. In 1526, Tyndale's New Testament became the first edition of the scriptures to be printed in the English language. This was good! If people could have access to read the Bible in their own language, the Catholic Church would no longer have a hold or dominion over them. The darkness of fear that controlled the people was no longer a threat. The public would get to challenge the church authority for any revealed lie.

Freedom had finally come; Salvation was free to all through faith and not works. It will always be the Word of God that is true, not man's. God's Word is true and the Truth shall set you free.

King James VI:

In 1603 when James VI became king there was a pending draft for a new translation of the Bible. The reason for the new translation was because The Great Bible, Mathew's Bible, Bishop's Bible, Geneva Bible, and Coverdale Bible, in use, were corrupted. At the Hampton Court Conference King James approved for the translation of the Bible. Forty-seven Bible Scholars, theologians and linguists were carefully chosen for this great work of translation. The Translators were divided into six groups and worked at Universities of Westminster, Cambridge, and Oxford. The different Books of the Bible were assigned to these Hebrew, Greek, Latin and English scholars. There were certain guidelines that had to be followed in order for this translation to take place. The translation of the Holy Bible from the original tongues was completed in 1611 and spread all around the world.

Plan 1: At first, In Egypt Alexandria, Satan attacked the Word of God

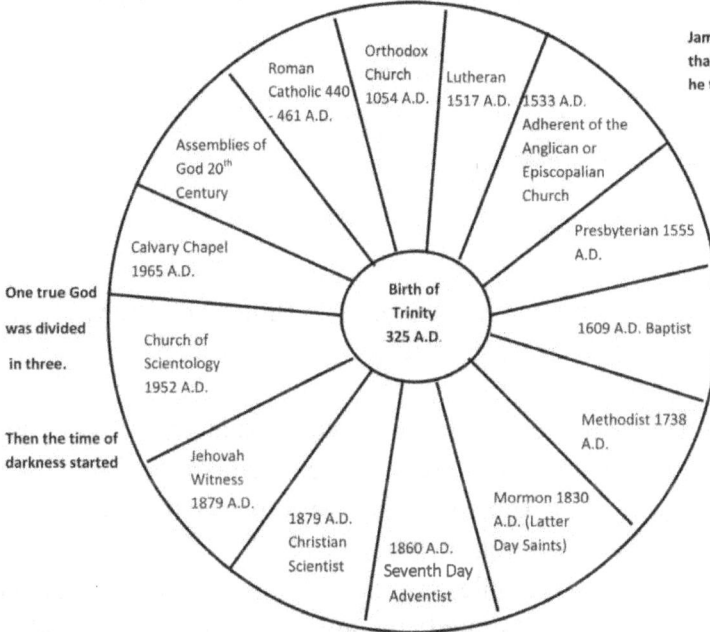

James 2:19 Satan knows that there is One God and he trembles.

Plan 2: Divide and Rule. Steal, Kill and Destroy. (John 10:10)

Bible says:

To know Jesus is REVELATION

(Mathew 16:13-19)

One true God was divided in three.

Then the time of darkness started

(circle diagram)

Orthodox Church 1054 A.D.
Roman Catholic 440 - 461 A.D.
Lutheran 1517 A.D.
1533 A.D. Adherent of the Anglican or Episcopalian Church
Assemblies of God 20th Century
Presbyterian 1555 A.D.
Calvary Chapel 1965 A.D.
Birth of Trinity 325 A.D.
1609 A.D. Baptist
Church of Scientology 1952 A.D.
Methodist 1738 A.D.
Jehovah Witness 1879 A.D.
Mormon 1830 A.D. (Latter Day Saints)
1879 A.D. Christian Scientist
1860 A.D. Seventh Day Adventist

AS A RESULT WE HAVE MANY DENOMINATIONS.

C.
Bible Translations Of Our Time:

T he Truth about different versions of The Bible: The Word of God is the Final Authority for our life.

At the present time, there are many different translations of the Bible besides the King James Version (KJV). The true followers of Christ would like to know if all the Bible versions are correct or not. Let us look for the truth in all these different versions of the Bible. We have NIV, NKJV, Catholic Bible, Latin Bible, American Standard Version, Revised Standard Version, English Standard Version, New American Standard Version, International Standard Version, Greek, and Hebrew Bible, and New World Translation (Jehovah's Witness) Bible etc. Also there are many other Bibles translated at different times and eras by many different scholars. How do we know that all these different versions are correct or have been corrupted? If corrupted, then how and when did it happen?

Let's begin our journey through these many variations to find the truth:

What we need to know is, to be able to determine which one is the true version:

The recent discovery of the Alexandria Original Script has a line, lines, or dashes over words and scriptures. This meant to omit those particular words and verses from their translation. They found these lines over words such as: Holy, Christ, and Spirit, along with many other words and verses. The Scribes who had the job of editing these manuscripts did not believe in the Lord Jesus Christ as the Messiah (Saviour). Whoever did the editing remove and changed many words and scriptures. This manuscript has recently been discovered in Alexandria, Egypt.

This is a wonderful proof that the Bible was changed and corrupted in Alexandria by their corrupted religious and political leaders.

King James Version of the Bible says:

All scripture is given by inspiration of God, and is profitable for doctrine, for reproof, for correction, for instruction in righteousness: (2 Tim 3:16 KJV)

Knowing this first, that no prophecy of the scripture is of any private interpretation. For the prophecy came not in old time by the will of man: but holy men of God spake as they were moved by the Holy Ghost. (2 Peter 1: 20-21)

This true word of God written by the one and only God.

The Word of God is eternal:

For verily I say unto you, till heaven and earth pass, one jot or one tittle shall in no wise pass from the law, till all be fulfilled. (Matthew 5:18)

And it is easier for heaven and earth to pass, than one tittle of the law to fail. (Luke 16:17)

Do not add or subtract to the Word of God:

The Word of God can't be subtracted, added, or misrepresented:

For I testify unto every man that heareth the words of the prophecy of this book, If any man shall add unto these things, God shall add unto him the plagues that are written in this book: And if any man shall take away from the words of the book of this prophecy, God shall take away his part out of the book of life, and out of the holy city, and from the things which are written in this book. (Revelation 22:18-19)

Ye shall not add unto the word which I command you, neither shall ye diminish ought from it, that ye may keep the commandments of the LORD your God which I command you. (Deuteronomy 4:2)

The Word of God is alive and sharper then a two edged sword:

Every Word of God is <u>pure</u>: He is a shield unto them that put their trust in him. (Proverb 30:5)

Psalms 119 tells us that the Word of God helps us to stay pure and grow in faith. The Word of God is the only guide for living a pure life.

*Thy word is a **<u>lamp</u>** unto my feet, and a **<u>light</u>** unto my path. (Psalms 119:105)*

*Being born again, not of corruptible seed, but of incorruptible, by **<u>the word of God</u>**, which liveth and abideth forever. (1 Peter 1:23)*

Of the many English Versions available today, only the King James Version (1611) without fail follows the superior Traditional Masoretic Hebrew text. This meticulous method was used by the Masorites in making copies of the Old Testament. Trustworthy proof of God's promise to preserve His Word, has never failed.

God is going to preserve His Word:

*The words of the LORD are **pure words**: as silver tried in a furnace of earth, purified seven times. Thou shalt keep them, O LORD, **thou shalt preserve them from this generation forever**. (Psalms 12:6, 7)*

Today's technology has proved how accurate and true the King James Version Bible is.

The Journal of Royal Statistical Society and Statistical Science is a new research agency:

Hebrew scholars, two Harvard and two Yale mathematicians, took these two statistical scientific techniques and were amazed by the accuracy of the KJV Bible. They did a computer informational study using the equidistant letter sequencing. They entered a name from the first five Books (Torah) of the KJV Bible and upon entering that name, the equidistant letter sequencing test was able to automatically populate that persons' date of birth, death and the city where they were born and died. They found this to be the most accurate report. It noted people who lived in the early century with ease and exact results. These were simple tests, but the findings flowed with great accuracy.

The same technique failed when they put the names used in the NIV, New American Standard Version, The Living Bible and other languages and translations from these versions. This method proves the inaccuracy of corrupted copies of the Bible.

They tried the same mathematical analysis for Samaritan Pentateuch, as well as the Alexandria Version and it did not work either.

The Book of Revelation tells us that:

And if any man shall take away from the words of the book of this prophecy, God shall take away his part out of the book of life, and out of the holy city, and from the things which are written in this book. (Revelation 22:19)

With this study, they came to the conclusion that the KJV Bible is the most truthful Bible that we have today.

A Greek Text based on the Masoretic Text and Textus Receptus: (simply means texts received by all) which was originally written underlies the KJV Bible. Over five thousand manuscripts agree 99% with the KJV Bible.

The KJV Bible is a public domain and needs no permission to be used for translation.

The Modern Bible versions do not use the Hebrew Masoretic Text. They have used Leningrad Manuscript, edited by the Septuagint a corrupt Greek version of the Old Testament. Both of these false Biblia Hebraica Hebrew texts offer in their own footnotes suggested changes. False Hebrew texts, BHK or BHS, are used for the Old Testament in all of the modern versions for translations.

The Traditional Masoretic Hebrew text that underlies the KJV is exactly the same to the original manuscript. Today, Archeologists have found all the books of the Bible which proves that the KJV Bible is the exact translation of the original Book.

The Word of God has changed:

The Bible says the word of God is our sword and is used as the only weapon of offence against the enemy; however, in modern translations, the Word of God can't be used as an offence or sword against the enemy. There have been so many changes in the Word of God that when we see the person who uses the modern translations, they are unstable, depressed, anxious and have emotional problems.

This is why Psychology and medicine has entered the church; new translations are responsible for this cause.

Let us see a few changes and the subtle reason behind it:

We will see changes in the following Versions of the Bible. I am mentioning a few of the versions but there are many other versions and translations done from this Bible which you can do your own research on as well. New Living Translation, English Standard Version, New American Standard Bible, International Standard Version, American Standard Version, Jehovah's Witness Bible and NIV Bible and other translations.

*KJV: Luke 4:18 The Spirit of the Lord [is] upon me, because he hath anointed me to preach the gospel to the poor; he hath sent me to **heal the brokenhearted**, to preach deliverance to the captives, and recovering of sight to the blind, to set at liberty them that are bruised,*

This scripture says that He heals the broken hearted.

The NIV reads Luke 4:18 "The Spirit of the Lord is on me, because he has anointed me to preach good news to the poor. He has sent me to proclaim freedom for the prisoners and recovery of sight for the blind, to release the oppressed;

(Heal the brokenhearted is omitted from the NIV and other versions as well. Modern translations can't heal the broken heart.)

*KJV: Mark 3:15: And to have **power to heal sicknesses**, and to cast out devils:*

NIV: Mark 3:15: And to have authority to drive out demons.

(**"And to have power to heal sicknesses"** is omitted from NIV and other translations. You are powerless to heal the sick.)

*KJV: Acts 3:11 And as the **lame man which was healed** held Peter and John, all the people ran together unto them in the porch that is called Solomon's, greatly wondering.*

NIV: Acts 3:11: While the beggar held on to Peter and John, all the people were astonished and came running to them in the place called Solomon's Colonnade.

The NIV Bible has removed: "**Lame man which was healed**" which is the key verse.

In addition to this the NIV has removed "Mercy Seat" fifty-three times. The Mercy of God Is omitted. The word Blood has been omitted forty-one times.

Ephesians 6:4 talking about nurturing the church...The word Nurturing derives from the word Nurse. Like holding and taking care of a baby, God nurtures us and humbles us, but some modern versions say, "discipline" and "chastening".

*The KJV Daniel 3:25b says: and the form of the fourth is like the **Son of God**.*

*NIV Daniel 3:25b: has changed the words; and the fourth looks like a **son of the gods**."*

Son of God is not son of gods...this will support polytheism.

By changing "The" to "A" will support other religions. Example: A gospel, a son, a savior....JESUS IS NOT THE ONLY SAVIOR?!?!?

The Bible Says:

Jesus saith unto him, I am the way, the truth, and the life: no man cometh unto the Father, but by me. (KJV John 14:6)

*KJV: Mathew 25:31: When the Son of man shall come in his glory, and all the **holy angels** with him, then shall he sit upon the throne of his glory.*

*NIV: Mathew 25:31: When the Son of Man comes in his glory, and all **the angels** with him, he will sit on his throne in heavenly glory*

(NIV has removed the word "Holy". We know that the Bible also talks about wicked and unholy Angels)

God is Holy:

NIV has also removed Holy Ghost or Holy Spirit from some places. These are just a few examples of many changes of NIV, NKJV, Catholic Bible, Latin Bible, American Standard Version, Revised Standard Version, Greek and Hebrew Bible and also other versions of the Bible, which were translated from old, corrupted Alexandrian Script and NIV.

The Following Proves That The NIV Bible Is Antichrist:

Many Words such as Jesus Christ or Christ, Messiah, Lord, etc. has been removed from NIV and other translations of the Bible. The Bible Says who the Antichrist is.

Antichrist:

Who is a liar but he that denieth that Jesus is the Christ? He is antichrist, that denieth the Father and the Son. (KJV 1 John 2:22)

*The grace of our Lord **Jesus Christ** [be] with you all. Amen. (KJV: Revelation 22:21)*

*The grace of the Lord Jesus be with God's people. Amen. (NIV: Revelation 22:21 has removed **Christ**.)*

KJV John 4:29: Come, see a man, which told me all things that ever I did: is not this the Christ?

NIV says John 4:29 "Come, see a man who told me everything I ever did. Could this be the Christ?"

(Deity of Christ is questioned) By removing words, the meaning is changed.

Antichrist denies Father and Son...

*KJV: John 9:35 "thou believe on **Son of God**".*

*NIV: Changed to "Do you believe in the **Son of Man**".*

KJV Acts 8:37 "And Philip said, If thou believest with all thine heart, thou mayest. And he answered and said, I believe that Jesus Christ is the Son of God."

Acts 8:37; entire verse is removed from NIV

*KJV: Galatians 4:7 wherefore thou art no more a servant, but a son; and if a son, then an heir of **God through Christ***

NIV: Galatians 4:7 so you are no longer a slave, but a son; and since you are a son, God has made you also an heir.

NIV omitted heir of God through Christ.

*KJV: Ephesians 3:9 And to make all [men] see what [is] the fellowship of the mystery, which from the beginning of the world hath been hid in God, who created all things **by Jesus Christ**:*

NIV: Ephesians 3:9 and to make plain to everyone the administration of this mystery, which for ages past was kept hidden in God, who created all things.

NIV has removed **"By Jesus Christ".** Jesus is the Creator of all things.

Jesus Christ comes in the flesh:

*1 John 4:3 KJV...And every spirit that confesseth not that **Jesus Christ is come in the flesh** is not of God.*

NIV says: But every spirit that does not acknowledge Jesus is not from God.

("Jesus Christ is come in the flesh" has been removed)

Book of Acts 3:13, 26 KJV says He is a Son of God. NKJV removed Son of God and said servant of God.

New Bible versions do not want Jesus to be the "Son of God". Son of God means God in flesh.

*John 5:17-18 KJV but Jesus answered them, **My Father** worketh hitherto, and I work. Therefore, the Jews sought the more to kill him, because he not only had broken the sabbath, but said also that **God was his Father**, making himself **equal with God***

The KJV Bible defines Jesus or Jesus Christ or The Lord Jesus. But new modern translations say "he or him" instead.

*KJV: And they sing the song of Moses the servant of God, and the song of the Lamb, saying, Great and marvellous [are] thy works, Lord God Almighty; just and true [are] thy ways, **thou King of saints**. (Revelation 15:3)*

*NIV: and sang the song of Moses the servant of God and the song of the Lamb: "Great and marvelous are your deeds, Lord God Almighty. Just and true are your ways, **King of the ages**. (Revelation 15:3)*

(He is the King of saints, who are born again. Who are baptized in the name of Jesus and received His Spirit.)

> * *KJV: And __God__ shall wipe away all tears from their eyes; (Revelation 21:4)*

NIV: __*He will*__ *wipe every tear from their eyes. (Revelation 21:4)*

"**God**" is changed to "He". Who is "He"? (This will support other religions.)

KJV: And I looked, and, lo, a Lamb stood on the mount Zion, and with him an hundred forty [and] four thousand, having his __Father's name__ written in their foreheads. (Revelation 14:1)

NIV: Then I looked, and there before me was the Lamb, standing on Mount Zion, and with him 144,000 who had __his name and his Father's name__ written on their foreheads. (Revelation14: 1)

NIV has added "His name" with "His Father's name" now two names.

John 5:43b: I am come in my Father's name.

So the name of the Father is Jesus. Jesus in the Hebrew language means Jehovah Savior

Zechariah 14:9 And the LORD shall be king over all the earth: in that day shall there be one LORD, and his __name one__

KJV Isaiah 44:5 One shall say, I am the Lord's; and another shall call himself by the name of Jacob; and another shall subscribe with his hand unto the Lord, and __surname__ himself by the name of Israel.

NIV: Isaiah 44:5 One will say, 'I belong to the LORD'; another will call himself by the name of Jacob; still another will write on his hand, 'The LORD's,' and will take the name Israel.

(NIV Removed the word **Surname**)

Now we hear that the book of the "Shepherd of Hermas" is going to be introduced into the modern version of the Bible. The Book of Hermas says, "Take the name, give up to the beast, form a one world government, and kill those who do not receive The Name. (Jesus is not the name they are referring to here)

KJV Revelation 13:17: And that no man might buy or sell, save he that had the mark, or the name of the beast, or the number of his name.

And do not be surprised if the Book of Revelation disappears from the Bible. Now, the Book of Revelation is where the past, present, and things to come are recorded. The Shepherd of Hermas is in the Sinaiticus Manuscript, which underlies the NIV Bible.

Symbols:

What is the meaning of symbol and who uses this symbol:
A **symbol** is something such as a particular mark that represents some piece of information for example; a red octagon may be a symbol for "STOP". On a map, a picture of a tent might represent a campsite.

666 =

Book of prophecy says:

Here is wisdom. Let him that hath understanding count the number of the beast: for it is the number of a man; and his number is Six hundred threescore and six. (Revelation 13:18)

This symbol or Logo of an interwoven 666 (ancient trinity symbol) is used by the people who believe in the Trinitarian doctrine.

God is not the trinity or three different persons. One God Jehovah came in the flesh and now His Spirit is working in the Church. God is One, will always be One.

But Acts 17:29 says: Forasmuch then as we are the offspring of God, we ought not to think that the Godhead is like unto gold, or silver, or stone, graven by art and man's device.

(To make a symbol to represent the Godhead is against the Word of God) New Agers admit that three inter-woven sixes or "666" is a mark of the Beast.

The Bible warns us that Satan is Counterfeit:

"And no marvel; for Satan himself is transformed into an angel of light. Therefore, it is no great thing if his Ministers also be transformed as the ministers of righteousness;" (2 Corinthians 11:14-15)

Satan is ultimately a counterfeit:

I will ascend above the heights of the clouds; I will be like the most High. (Isaiah 14:14)

I will be like the most High God. It is obvious that Satan has tried to take away the identity of Jesus Christ by changing The Word of God. Remember Satan is subtle and his attack is on "The Word of God".

New King James Version:

Let us see this Version of the Bible called NKJV. New King James Version is **not** a King James Version. King James Version Bible was translated by 54 Hebrew Greek and Latin Theologian Scholars, in 1611.

The New King James Version was first published in 1979. By studying the New KJV we will find out that this Version is not only the deadliest but very deceiving to the body of Christ.

Why??????

The NKJV publisher says:

.... That it's a King James Bible which is not true. KJV has no copy right; you can translate it into any language without getting permission. NKJV has a copy right owned by Thomas Nelson Publishers.

.... That it's based on the Textus Receptus, which is only partial truth. This is another subtle attack. Be careful about this New KJV. You will find out in a minute as to why.

The New King James Bible claims to be King James Bible, only better. The "NKJV", has omitted and altered many verses.

Twenty-two times "Hell" is changed to "Hades" and "Sheol". The New age satanic movement says "Hades" is a midway state of purification!

Greek people believe "Hades" and "Sheol" is an underground abode of the dead.

There are many deletions of the following words: repent, God, Lord, heaven, and blood. The words Jehovah, devils, and damnation, and New Testament is removed from the NKJV.

Misunderstandings About Salvation:

KJV	NKJV
1st Corinthians 1:18	
"Are saved"	Being saved.
Hebrew 10:14	
"Are sanctified"	Are being sanctified.
II Corinthians 10:5	
"Casting down imaginations"	Casting down arguments.
Matthew 7:14	

"Narrow way" II	Difficult way
Corinthians 2:15	
"Are Saved"	Being saved

"Sodomites" is changed, to "perverted persons." The NKJV is an antichrist misrepresented version

Satan's biggest attack is on Jesus as God.

NIV: Isaiah 14:12 is a subtle attack on the Lord Jesus who is known as **Morning Star.**

How you have fallen from heaven, O morning star, son of the dawn! You have been cast down to the earth, you who once laid low the nations!

(NIV has Foot Notes for this scripture *2 Peter 1:19 "And we have the word of the prophets made more certain, and you will do well to pay attention to it, as to a light shining in a dark place, until the day dawns and the morning star rises in your hearts."*

By adding *__Morning Star__* and giving another reference in Revelation 2:28 misguides the reader, that Jesus is the Morning Star, who has fallen.)

But KJV Isaiah 14:12 reads, "How art thou fallen from heaven, O Lucifer, son of the morning! [how] art thou cut down to the ground, which didst weaken the nations!"

(The NIV bible has removed Lucifer's name and replaced "son of the morning" with "**Morning Star.**" In the book of Revelations Jesus is referred to as "The Morning Star."

I Jesus have sent mine angel to testify unto you these things in the churches. I am the root and the offspring of David, and the bright and morning star (KJV 22:16).

Thus, the NIV version of Isaiah 14:12 misconstrues the biblical meaning by stating that Jesus has fallen from heaven and laid low the nations.) The KJV Bible says Jesus is the Bright and Morning Star.

*"I Jesus have sent mine angel to testify unto you these things in the Churches. I am the root and the offspring of David, and the **bright and Morning star.**" (Revelation 22:16 KJV)*

KJV:

We have also a more sure word of prophecy; whereunto ye do well that ye take heed, as unto a light that shineth in a dark place, until the day dawn, and the day star arise in your hearts: (KJV 2 Peter 1:19)

*And he shall rule them with a rod of iron; as the vessels of a potter shall they be broken to shivers: even as I received of my Father. And I will give him the **morning star.** (KJV Rev. 2:27-28)*

Modern day translations accommodate all religions by using 'he' or 'him' instead of Jesus, Christ or Messiah, and by removing many words and verses about Jesus. These translations prove that the Lord Jesus is not the Creator, the Savior, or the God in the Flesh; they make Him just another myth.

These apostate men produced a manuscript for a Bible more to their own liking. They attacked the deity of Jesus Christ and other doctrines in the Bible. The way was paved for a New Age Bible to give birth to one world religion. The joining together of all churches and all religions, will bring "One World Religion".

Now you understand what conniving and subtle plan Satan has designed. He even dared to change the Word of God. Satan developed a deceiving plan to confuse people!

Remember what Satan said:

I will ascend above the heights of the clouds; I will be like the most High. (Isaiah 14:14)

D.
KJV Vs Modern Bible: Changes That Have Been Added Or Taken away.

NIV TRANSLATION:

The Greek text of Westcott & Hort comes from the Sinaiticus and Vaticanus manuscripts. The early church found it to be a subtle attack on the Word of God by omitting and changing the truth of the Bible. Sinaiticus(Aleph) and Vaticanus(Codex-B) both have been rejected by the early church and admired by false teachers. The source of the NIV Bible is based on the Westcott & Hort corrupted versions which you will find in the NIV foot notes. We don't have any way of knowing how and where this Greek text of Westcott & Hort originated, without extensive research. When we see references given from Westcott and Hort, we usually believe them without question, simply because they are printed in a Bible.

The NIV Bible is admired because people believe it is easier to understand since the old English has been changed to modern day words. As a matter of fact, the KJV Bible has the easiest language that can be understood by any age. The KJV vocabulary is simpler than the NIV vocabulary. Just by changing words like thee, thy, thou, and thine, people think it is easier to read. As you know, the Word of God is only explained by the Holy Spirit, which is written by God. The Spirit of God is in the KJV which helps us to grasp His understanding. Changes are not needed in God's Word; however the true Word needs to change our thinking.

So many churches are now accepting the NIV version in place of the KJV. Making small changes over time conditions our thinking and it becomes a subtle way of brain washing. The changes that the NIV Bible has made to their version, is subtly diluting the Gospel. These changes are mostly against the Lordship of the Lord Jesus Christ. Once this is accomplished, many religions find it easier to accept the NIV Bible because it then supports their doctrines. This in turn becomes "interfaithism", the goal of the one world religion spoken of in Revelation.

The KJV was based off the Byzantine family of manuscripts which were commonly called the Textus Receptus manuscripts. The NKJV (New King James Version) is the worst translation. It differs from the KJV 1200 times. The New King James version is definitely not the same as the King James Version. The MKJV also is not the KJV. The majority of Bible translations are not another version but a perversion, and are deviated from the truth.

The following verses are not in the **NIV** and **other modern translations**. The following is a list of "omissions" in the NIV.

Isaiah 14:12

*KJV: Isa.14:12: How art thou fallen from heaven, **O Lucifer**, **son of the morning**! How art thou cut down to the ground, which didst weaken the nations!*

*NIV Isa.14:12 how you have fallen from heaven, o **morning star**, son of the dawn! You have been cast down to the earth, you who once laid low the nations!*

(The NIV Bible has taken out Lucifer and replaced "son of the morning star" with "Morning star". This is misleading you to believe that, "JESUS" who is the "MORNING STAR"; has fallen from heaven.

I Jesus have sent mine angel to testify unto you these things in the churches. I am the root and the offspring of David, and the bright and __morning star__. (KJV Revelation 22: 16)

(Jesus is the morning star)

Isaiah 14:12 (NIV), is a very confusing scripture. People think Jesus is fallen from heaven and cut down.

The NIV makes Lucifer (Satan) equal to Jesus Christ; this is blasphemy of the highest order. This is why some people don't believe in Jesus Christ since they see him equal to Satan.

Daniel 3:25

KJV: Dan.3:25 He answered and said, Lo, I see four men loose, walking in the midst of the fire, and they have no hurt; and the form of the fourth is like the __Son of God__.

NIV: Dan. 3:25 He said, "Look! I see four men walking around in the fire, unbound and unharmed, and the fourth looks like a __son of the gods__."

(Changing Son of God to __Son of the gods__ will accommodate the belief of polytheism, and this will support other religions.)

Matthew 5:22

KJV Mt.5:22 But I say unto you, that whosoever is __angry with his brother without a cause__ shall be in danger of the judgment: and whosoever shall say to his brother, Raca, shall be in danger of the council: but whosoever shall say, Thou fool, shall be in danger of hell fire.

NIV Mt.5:22 But I tell you that anyone who is **angry** *with his brother will be subject to judgment. Again, anyone who says to his brother, 'Raca,' is* **answerable to the Sanhedrin**. *But anyone who says, 'You fool!' will be in danger of the fire of hell.*

(KJV Bible says, **angry without a cause** NIV says just angry. The Truth of the Word is, we can get **angry** if there is cause, but will not let the sun set on it.)

Matthew 5:44

KJV Mt.5:44 But I say unto you, Love your enemies, **bless them that curse you**, *do good to them that hate you, and pray* **for them which despitefully use you**, *and persecute you;*

NIV Mt.5:44 But I tell you, love your enemies and pray for those who persecute you,

(Highlighted in KJV is removed from the NIV Bible)

Matthew 6:13

KJV Mt. 6:13 And lead us not into temptation, but deliver us from evil: **For thine is the kingdom, and the power, and the glory, for ever. Amen.**

NIV Mt. 6:13 And lead us not into temptation, but deliver us from the **evil one**.

(**Evil** not evil one. **For thine is the kingdom, and the power, and the glory, forever. Amen**: removed from NIV)

Matthew 6:33

*KJV Mt 6:33 But seek ye first the **kingdom of God**, and his righteousness; and all these things shall be added unto you.*

*NIV Mt 6:33 But seek first his kingdom and **his** righteousness, and all these things will be given to you as well.*

(**the kingdom of God** is replaced by "his" kingdom...NIV replaced God for his. Who is "His"?)

Matthew 8:29

*KJV Mt.8:29 And, behold, they cried out, saying, What have we to do with thee, **Jesus**, thou Son of God? art thou come hither to torment us before the time? (Specific)*

*NIV Mt.8:29 "What do you want with us, **Son of God**?" they shouted. "Have you come here to torture us before the appointed time?"*

(**Jesus** is out of the NIV Bible and they only kept Son of God...*Jesus* is the Son of God. Son of God means the Almighty God walking in flesh.)

Matthew 9:13b

*KJV Mt.9:13b for I am not come to call the righteous, but sinners to **repentance**.*

NIV Mt.9:13b for I have not come to call the righteous, but sinners.

(**To repentance** is out. Repentance is the first step; you are turning from sin and a sinful life style by realizing and confessing you were wrong.)

Matthew 9:18

*KJV: Mt 9:18 While he spake these things unto them, behold, there came a certain ruler, and **worshipped him**, saying, My daughter is even now dead: but come and lay thy hand upon her, and she shall live.*

(Worshipped Jesus)

*NIV Mt 9:18 While he was saying this, a ruler came and **knelt before him** and said, "My daughter has just died. But come and put your hand on her, and she will live."*

(Worship is **changed to knelt**. Worship makes Jesus as God.)

Matthew 13:51

*KJV Mt 13:51 Jesus saith unto them, Have ye understood all these things? They say unto him, **Yea, Lord**.*

NIV Mt 13:51 "Have you understood all these things?" Jesus asked.

(JESUS IS THE LORD. The NIV took out **Yea Lord**; Leaving out Jesus Christ's Lordship)

Matthew 16:20

*KJV Mt 16:20 Then charged he his disciples that they should tell no man that he was **Jesus** the Christ.*

(The name "JESUS" is removed from several verses of the NIV Bible.)

NIV Mt 16:20 Then he warned his disciples not to tell anyone that he was the Christ.

(Who is "he"? Why not Jesus, the Christ? "Christ" means Messiah, the Saviour of this world: John 4:42.)

Matthew 17:21

KJV: Mt 17:21: Howbeit this kind goeth not out but by prayer and fasting.

(Prayer and fasting will pull down the Devil's strong hold. Fasting kills our flesh.)

NIV took out the scripture completly. It is also deleted from the Jehovah's Witness "Bible". Present time fasting is changed to Daniels diet. This is another lie. (Fasting is no food and no water. Eating is not fasting and fasting is not eating or drinking)

Few Examples of Biblical Fasting in KJV Bible

Esther 4:16 KJV:

*Go, gather together all the Jews that are present in Shushan, and **fast** ye for me, and **neither eat nor drink three** days, night or day: I also and my maidens will **fast** likewise; and so will I go in unto the king, which is not according to the law: and if I perish, I perish*

*Jonah 3:5, 7 KJV So the people of Nineveh believed God,and **proclaimed a fast**, and put on sackcloth, from the greatest of them even to the least of them. And he caused it to be proclaimed and published through Nineveh by the decree of the king and his nobles, saying ,Let neither man nor beast, herd nor flock, **taste any thing: let them not feed, nor drink water**:*

Matthew 18:11

*KJV Mt 18:11: **For the Son of man is come to save that which was lost**.*

(This verse is deleted from The NIV and many other versions of the Bible. Jesus is not to be the only Savior. Mason teaches we can save ourselves and you do not need Jesus.)

Matthew 19:9

*KJV: Mt 19:9: And I say unto you, whosoever shall put away his wife, except it be for fornication, and shall marry another, committeth adultery: **and who so marrieth her which is put away doth commit adultery.***

NIV: Mt 19:9 I tell you that anyone who divorces his wife, except for marital unfaithfulness, and marries another woman commits adultery."

("who so marrieth her which is put away doth commit adultery;" is omitted)

Matthew 19:16,17

*KJV Mt 19:16 And, behold, one came and said unto him, **Good Master**, what good thing shall I do, that I may have eternal life?*

17 And he said unto him, Why callest thou me good? There is none good but one, that is, God: but if thou wilt enter into life, keep the commandments.

NIV Mt 19:16 Now a man came up to Jesus and asked, "Teacher, what good thing must I do to get eternal life?

17 "Why do you ask me about what is good?" Jesus replied. "There is only one who is good. If you want to enter life, keep the commandments.

(Jesus said, "Why do you call me good?" Only God is good and if Jesus is good then he must be God. Good Master is changed to "Teacher" in the NIV and the meaning is lost. Also some religion supports the belief of self-saving.)

Matthew 20:16

*KJV Mt 20:16: So the last shall be first, and the first last: **for many be called, but few chosen**.*

(It is important what we choose. You could get lost if you do not choose correctly)

NIV AND RSV

NIV Mt. 20:16:" So the last will be first, and the first will be last."

(do not care to choose)

Matthew 20:20

*KJV Mt 20:20: Then came to him the mother of Zebedees children with her sons, **worshipping him**, and desiring a certain thing of him.*

*NIV Mt 20:20: Then the mother of Zebedee's sons came to Jesus with her sons and, **kneeling down**, asked a favor of him.*

(**Worship or kneeling down…?**: Leaving out Jesus Christ's Lordship, Jews only worship One God)

Matthew 20:22, 23

*KJV Mt 20:22, 23: But Jesus answered and said, Ye know not what ye ask. Are ye able to drink of the cup that I shall drink of, and to be **baptized with the baptism that I am baptized with**? They say unto him, we are able.*

*And he saith unto them, Ye shall drink indeed of my cup, and be **baptized with the baptism that I am baptized with**: but to sit on my*

217

right hand, and on my left, is not mine to give, but it shall be given to them for whom it is prepared of my Father.

(Could you go through the suffering that I went through?)

NIV Mt 20:22, 23: "You don't know what you are asking," Jesus said to them. "Can you drink the cup I am going to drink?" " We can," they answered. Jesus said to them, "You will indeed drink from my cup, but to sit at my right or left is not for me to grant. These places belong to those for whom they have been prepared by my Father."

(All highlighted and underlined phrases in KJV has been removed from NIV)

Matthew 21:44

*KJV Mt 21:44: And whosoever shall fall on this stone shall be broken: but on whomsoever it shall fall, it will **grind him to powder**.*

*NIV Mt 21:44: He who falls on this stone will be broken **to pieces**, but he on whom it falls will be crushed."*

(Grind him to powder has been removed)

Matthew 23:10

*KJV Mt 23:10: Neither be ye called **masters**: for one is your **Master**, even **Christ**.*

NIV Mt 23:10: Nor are you to be called 'teacher,' for you have one Teacher, the Christ.

(You have to bring God down to the level of mystics so that Jesus becomes another mystic. The truth is Christ satisfies all.)

Matthew 23:14

KJV: Mt 23:14: Woe unto you, scribes and Pharisees, hypocrites! For ye devour widows' houses, and for a pretence make long prayer: therefore ye shall receive the greater damnation.

(NIV, New L T, English Standard Version New American Standard Bible and New world translations have this verse deleted. Check it out for yourself in your Bible.)

Matthew 24:36

KJV: Mt 24:36: But of that day and hour knoweth no man, no, not the angels of heaven, but my Father only.

*NIV: Mt 24:36: "No one knows about that day or hour, not even the angels in heaven, **nor the Son**, but only the Father.*

("nor the son" is added in the NIV Bible. John 10: 30 **I and my Father are one**. So Jesus knows His coming time. This implies Jesus is not in the Godhead. But in those days, after that tribulation, the sun shall be darkened, and the moon shall not give her light, Mark 13:24. It will be hard to tell the time.)

Matthew 25:13

*KJV: Mt 25:13 Watch therefore, for ye know neither the day nor the hour **wherein the Son of man cometh**.*

NIV: Mt 25:13 "Therefore keep watch, because you do not know the day or the hour."

(**"Wherein the Son of man cometh**." Leaving out who is coming back? What watch of?)

Matthew 25:31

KJV: Mt 25:31When the Son of man shall come in his glory, and all the **holy angels** *with him, then shall he sit upon the throne of his glory*

NIV: Mt 25:31 "When the Son of man comes in his glory, and all the **angels** *with him, he will sit on his throne in heavenly glory."*

(KJV says all the "holy" angels. NIV says just "the angels." This implies that the fallen or unholy angels are coming with Jesus. Doesn't it? There is a heresy going around that it doesn't matter what you do good or bad, you still go to heaven. Spirits of our dead loved ones who never believed in Jesus, are supposed to come back to tell their loved ones that they are okay in heaven, and you don't have to do anything to get into heaven. This is a doctrine of the devil.)

Matthew 27:35

KJV MT 27:35: And they crucified him, and parted his garments, casting lots: **_that it might be fulfilled which was spoken by the prophet, they parted my garments among them, and upon my vesture did they cast lots._**

NIV MT 27:35: When they had crucified him, they divided up   his clothes by casting lots.

("that it might be fulfilled which was spoken by the prophet, they parted my garments among them, and upon my vesture did they cast lots." Completely taken out of NIV Bible)

Mark 1:14

KJV MARK 1:14: Now after that John was put in prison, Jesus came into Galilee, **_preaching the gospel of the kingdom of God_**

NIV MARK 1:14: After John was put in prison, Jesus went into Galilee, __proclaiming the good news of God.__

(Gospel of the Kingdom of God is left out from NIV)

Mark 2:17

KJV Mark 2:17: When Jesus heard it, he saith unto them, they that are whole have no need of the physician, but they that are sick: I came not to call the righteous, but sinners to __repentance__.

NIV Mark 2:17: On hearing this, Jesus said to them, "It is not the healthy who need a doctor, but the sick. I have not come to call the righteous, but sinners."

(As long as you believe it is ok, you can do whatever, and it is ok. By slightly changing the scripture Sin is welcome.)

Mark 5:6

KJV Mark 5:6: But when he saw Jesus afar off, he ran and __worshipped him__,

(He recognizes that Jesus is the Lord God.)

NIV Mark 5:6: When he saw Jesus from a distance, he ran and __fell on his knees in front of him.__

(He shows respect as a man but does not recognize him as Lord God.)

Mark 6:11

KJV: Mark 6:11 "And whosoever shall not receive you, nor hear you, when ye depart thence, shake off the dust under your feet for a testimony against them. __Verily I say unto you, it shall be more tolerable for Sodom and Gomorrah in the day of judgment, than for that city__.

Elizabeth Das

NIV Mark 6:11 "And if any place will not welcome you or listen to you, shake the dust off your feet when you leave, as a testimony against them."

(NIV has removed, "Verily I say unto you, it shall be more tolerable for Sodom and Gomorrah in the day of judgment, than for that city." Judgment is removed since they do not believe in it and it does not matter what choice you make. All wrong sayings and doings will be corrected in purgatory or reincarnation.)

Mark 7:16

KJV Mark 7:16: If any man have ears to hear, let him hear

(NIV, Jehovah's Witness Bible and modern translations has removed this scripture. WOW!)

Mark 9:24

*KJV Mark 9:24: And straightway the father of the child cried out, and said with tears, **Lord**, I believe; help thou mine unbelief.*

NIV Mark 9:24: Immediately the boy's father exclaimed, "I do believe; help me overcome my unbelief!"

(Lord is missing from NIV. Jesus Christ's Lordship is left out)

Mark 9:29

*KJV Mark 9:29: And he said unto them, This kind can come forth by nothing, but by prayer and **fasting**.*

NIV Mark 9: 29: He replied, "This kind can come out only by prayer."

(**Fasting** is removed. By fasting we pull down strong holds of Satan. Seeking the face of God by biblical fasting and prayer brings the special anointing and power.)

Mark 9 :44

KJV Mark 9:44: Where their worm dieth not, and the fire is not quenched.

(Scripture is removed form NIV, modern transition and Jehovah's Witness Bible. They do not believe in punishment in hell.)

Mark 9:46

KJV: Mark 9:46: Where their worm dieth not, and the fire is not quenched.

(Scripture is removed from the NIV, modern translation and Jehovah's Witness Bible. Again, they do not believe in judgment.)

Mark 10:21

*KJV Mark 10:21: Then Jesus beholding him loved him, and said unto him, One thing thou lackest: go thy way, sell whatsoever thou hast, and give to the poor, and thou shalt have treasure in heaven: and come **take up the cross**, and follow me.*

(Christian has a cross to carry. There is a change in your life.)

NIV Mark 10:21: Jesus looked at him and loved him. "One thing you lack," he said. "Go, sell everything you have and give to the poor, and you will have treasure in heaven. Then come, follow me."

(NIV has removed "take up the cross" no need to suffer for truth. Live the way you want to live. Cross is very important for the Christian walk.)

Mark 10 :24

*KJV Mark 10:24: And the disciples were astonished at his words. But Jesus answereth again, and saith unto them, Children, how hard is it for them **that trust in riches** to enter into the kingdom of God!*

NIV Mark 10:24: The disciples were amazed at his words. But Jesus said again, "Children, how hard it is to enter the kingdom of God!

("**that trust in riches**" is removed; no need of these words in the NIV Bible since they want alms. That also makes you feel that it's hard to enter the Kingdom of God and discourages you.)

Mark 11:10

*KJV Mark 11:10: Blessed be the kingdom of our father David, **that cometh in the name of the Lord**: Hosanna in the highest.*

*NIV Mark 11:10: "Blessed is **the coming kingdom** of our father David!" "Hosanna in the highest!"*

(NIV: "that cometh in the name of the Lord" is removed)

Mark 11:26

KJV: Mark 11:26 But if ye do not forgive, neither will your Father which is in heaven forgive your trespasses.

(This Scripture is completely removed from the NIV, Jehovah's Witness Bible, (called the New World translation) and many other modern translations. Forgiveness is very important, if you want to be forgiven.)

Mark 13 :14

*KJV Mark 13:14: But when ye shall see the abomination of desolation, **spoken of by Daniel the prophet**, standing where it ought not, (let him* *that readeth understand,) then let them that be in Judaea flee to the mountains:*

NIV Mark 13:14: "When you see 'the abomination that causes desolation' standing where it does not belong— let the reader understand—then let those who are in Judea flee to the mountains.

(Information about the Book of Daniel is removed from NIV. We study the end time in the Book of Daniel and Revelation. BLESSED ARE THOSE WHO READ THE WORDS OF THIS BOOK. Blessed is he that readeth, and they that hear the words of this **prophecy**, and keep those things which are written therein: for the time is at hand. (Revelation 1:3) By removing the name of Daniel, it leaves you confused)

Mark 15:28

KJV: Mark 15:28: And the scripture was fulfilled, which saith, and he was numbered with the transgressors.

(Removed from NIV, Jehovah's Witness Bible, and modern translations)

Luke 2:14

*KJV: Luke 2:14 Glory to God in the highest, and on earth peace, **good will toward men.***

NIV Luke 2:14: Glory to God in the highest, and on earth peace to men on whom his favor rests. "

(Subtle change. instead of "good will toward men;" The NIV Bible says peace only for certain people whom God favors. This is also against God's principle.)

Luke 2:33

*KJV Luke 2:33: And **Joseph** and his mother*

Elizabeth Das

NIV Luke 2:33: The child's father and mother.

(**Joseph** is removed)

Luke 4:4

*KJV Luke 4:4 And Jesus answered him, saying, it is written, That man shall not live by bread alone, **but by every word of God**.*

NIV Luke 4:4 Jesus answered, "It is written: 'Man shall not live on bread alone.'

Satan's attack is on the **WORD OF GOD** In Genesis 3: Satan attacked the WORD OF GOD. He has a subtle attack "**But by every word of God**" is removed from NIV

NIV and the modern translation of the Bible for foramtor does not care for the Word of God. They change the wording to fit their doctrine, on their partiality as to what they think it should say. The word of God is alive and brings conviction to one's self. When God convicts you of sin, it brings repentance. If the word of God has been altered, it cannot bring true conviction; therefore, no repentance will be sought. By doing this the NIV indicates all religion is ok, which we know is not true.

Luke 4:8

*KJV Luke 4:8 And Jesus answered and said unto him, **Get thee behind me, Satan**: for it is written, Thou shalt worship the Lord thy God, and him only shalt thou serve.*

(Jesus rebuked Satan. You and I can rebuke Satan in the name of Jesus.)

NIV Luke 4:8 Jesus answered, "It is written: 'Worship the Lord your God and serve him only

("**Get thee behind me, Satan**" is taken out from NIV.)

Luke 4:18

*KJV Luke 4:18: The Spirit of the Lord is upon me, because he hath anointed me to preach the gospel to the poor; he hath sent me to **heal the brokenhearted**, to preach deliverance to the captives, and recovering of sight to the blind, to set at liberty them that are bruised,*

NIV Luke 4:18 "The Spirit of the Lord is on me, because he has anointed me to proclaim good news to the poor. He has sent me to proclaim freedom for the prisoners and recovery of sight for the blind, to release the oppressed."

("**to heal the brokenhearted**"is removed from the NIV: People who use this corrupted version are generally, anxious, emotionally unstable, and depressed. Changing the Word of God takes away the power of the Word. Truth will make you free so they removed the truth from the modern Bible.)

Luke 4:41

*KJV Luke 4:41: And devils also came out of many, crying out, and saying, **Thou art Christ the Son of God**. And he rebuking them suffered them not to speak: for they knew that he was Christ.*

(Do men confess "Thou art Christ the Son of God?" No, unless it is revealed by His Spirit.)

*NIV Luke 4:41: Moreover, demons came out of many people, shouting, "**You are the Son of God**!" But he rebuked them and would not allow them to speak, because they knew he was the Christ.*

(By removing "**Christ**", the demon did not confess Christ as the Son of God. Satan does not want people to accept Jesus as Jehovah Savior, so they change the Word of God with deeper intention. The demon knew that Jesus is God in the flesh.)

Luke 8:48

*KJV Luke 8:48: And he said unto her, Daughter, **be of good comfort**: thy faith hath made thee whole; go in peace.*

NIV Luke 8:48: Then he said to her, "Daughter, your faith has healed you. Go in peace."

("Be of good comfort," is omitted from the NIV. So comfort is gone, you can't be comforted by reading the NIV Bible)

Luke 9:55

*KJV Luke 9:55: But he turned, and rebuked them, and said, **Ye know not what manner of spirit ye are of**.*

NIV Luke 9:55: But Jesus turned and rebuked them.

(NIV has removed these words: "**Ye know not what manner of spirit ye are of**.")

Luke 9:56

*KJV: Luke 9:56: For **the Son of man is not come to destroy men's lives, but to save them**. And they went to another village.*

NIV Luke 9:56 and they went to other village.

(NIV REMOVED: **The Son of man is not come to destroy men's lives, but to save them**. Reason of Jesus to come is destroyed by removing this part of the scripture.)

Luke 11:2-4

*KJV Luke 11:2-4: And he said unto them, **when ye pray, say, Our Father which art in heaven**, Hallowed be thy name. Thy kingdom* *come. __Thy will be done, as in heaven, so in earth__. Give us day by day our daily bread. And forgive us our sins; for we also forgive every one that is indebted to us. And lead us not into temptation; __but deliver us from evil__.*

NIV Luke 11:2-4: He said to them, "When you pray, say: "Father, hallowed be your name, your kingdom come. Give us each day our daily bread. Forgive us our sins, for we also forgive everyone who sins against us. And lead us not into temptation. "

(NIV is not specific.All highlighted from KJV is left out from NIV and other modern versions of the Bible)

Luke 17:36

KJV Luke 17:36 Two men shall be in the field; the one shall be taken, and the other left.

(NIV, Modern version, and Jehovah's Witness Bible has removed the complete scripture)

Luke 23:17

Luke 23:17: (For of necessity he must release one unto them at the feast.)

(NIV, Jehovah's Witness Bible and many modern Bible versions have removed the scripture completely.)

Luke 23:38

KJV Luke 23:38: And a superscription also was written over him __in letters of Greek, and Latin, and Hebrew__, THIS IS THE KING OF THE JEWS.

NIV Luke 23:38: There was a written notice above him, which read: THIS IS THE KING OF THE JEWS.

(NIV and other modern translations have removed: "**in letters of Greek, and Latin, and Hebrew,**" Removes the evidence of languages spoken at that time.)

Luke 23:42

*KJV Luke 23:42: And he said unto Jesus, **<u>Lord</u>**, remember me when thou comest into thy kingdom.*

(Thief realized that Jesus is Lord)

NIV Luke 23:42: Then he said, "Jesus, remember me when you come into your kingdom"

(Not wanting to recognize Jesus' Lordship)

Luke 24:42

*KJV Luke 24:42: And they gave him a piece of a broiled fish, and of a **<u>honeycomb</u>**.*

NIV Luke 24:42: They gave him a piece of a broiled fish.

(Modern day Bibles give half the information. "Honeycomb" missing from NIV and other versions of the Bible)

John 5:3

*KJV John 5:3: In these lay a great multitude of impotent folk, of blind, halt, withered, **<u>waiting for the moving of the water</u>***

NIV John 5:3: Here a great number of disabled people used to lie the blind, the lame, the paralyzed.

(They removed the information that a miracle was happening at that place "waiting for the moving of the water.")

John 5:4

KJV: John 5:4: For an angel went down at a certain season into the pool, and troubled the water: whosoever then first after the troubling of the water stepped in was made whole of whatsoever disease he had.

(NIV and modern translations along with the Jehovah's Witness Bible have removed the scripture completly.)

John 6:47

*KJV: John 6:47: Verily, verily, I say unto you, He that **believeth on me** hath everlasting life.*

NIV: John 6:47: I tell you the truth, he who believes has everlasting life.

(**Believeth on me** has been changed to **Believes**. Believe on who? The word Believeth has "eth" in the end which means the word is continual. Any word that has "eth" in the end, means it is continual, not just one time.)

John 8:9a

*KJV John 8:9a: And they which heard it, **being convicted by their own conscience**, went out.*

NIV John 8:9a: those who heard began to go away

(NIV has removed "**being convicted by their own conscience**" they do not believe in having a conscience.)

John 9:4a

*KJV John 9:4a: **I** must work the works of him that sent me.*

*NIV John 9:4a: **We** must do the work of him who sent me.*

(Jesus said "**I**" the NIV and a few other versions, changed "**I**" to "**WE**")

John 10:30

*KJV: John 10:30: I and **my** Father are one.*

NIV: John 10:30: I and the Father are one."

(I and my father are **one** not two. "My father" makes Jesus the Son of God. That means God in the flesh. NIV has removed "my" and changed the complete meaning of the scripture.)

John 16:16

*KJV: John 16:16: A little while, and ye shall not see me: and again, a little while, and ye shall see me, **because I go to the Father**.*

NIV: John 16:16: "In a little while you will see me no more, and then after a little while you will see me."

(NIV removed "because I go to the Father. Many religions believe that Jesus went to the Himalaya or another place and did not die.)

Acts 2:30

*KJV: Acts 2:30: Therefore, being a prophet, and knowing that God had sworn with an oath to him, that of the fruit of his loins, according to the flesh, **he would raise up Christ to sit on his throne**

NIV: Acts 2:30: But he was a prophet and knew that God had promised him on oath that he would place one of his descendants on his throne.

(**NIV has removed "he would raise up Christ to sit on his throne**" the prophecy about Jesus coming in the flesh is wiped out.)

Acts 3:11

*KJV: Acts3:11: And as the **lame man which was healed** held Peter and John, all the people ran together unto them in the porch that is called Solomon's, greatly wondering.*

NIV: Acts3:11: While the beggar held on to Peter and John, all the people were astonished and came running to them in the place called Solomon's Colonnade.

("**lame man which was healed**" is the key part of this scripture, NIV has removed this)

Acts 4:24

*KJV: Acts 4:24: And when they heard that, they lifted up their voice to God with one accord, and said, Lord, **thou art God**, which hast made heaven, and earth, and the sea, and all that in them is:*

NIV: Acts 4:24: When they heard this, they raised their voices together in prayer to God. "Sovereign Lord," they said, "you made the heaven and the earth and the sea, and everything in them

(NIV and modern translations removed "thou art God". Not confessing the one true God who did a miracle.)

Acts 8:37

KJV: Acts 8:37: And Philip said, If thou believest with all thine heart, thou mayest. And he answered and said, I believe that Jesus Christ is the Son of God.

(NIV and modern version Bibles has taken out the scripture completely)

The word "Master" from the KJV has been removed in the modern versions of the Bible and changed to "teacher" putting Jesus in the same class as all other teachers of different religions. The reason for this change is mainly due to the Ecumenical movement which states that you cannot put Jesus as the only way to salvation because it lowers all other faiths who don't believe Jesus is our one and only true Savior. Such for example Hindu's and most all other eastern religions.

Acts 9:5

*KJV Acts 9:5: And he said, Who art thou, Lord? And the Lord said, I am Jesus whom thou persecutest: **it is hard for thee to kick against the pricks**.*

NIV: Acts 9:5: Who are you, Lord?" Saul asked. "I am Jesus, whom you are persecuting," he replied.

(NIV and modern translations have removed the "**it is hard for thee to kick against the pricks**." That means by removing all this scripture they will not prevail.)

Acts 15:34

KJV: Acts 15:34: Notwithstanding it pleased Silas to abide there still.

(NIV Bible and other modern Bible translations took out the scripture.)

Acts 18:7

*KJV Acts 18:7: And he departed thence, and entered into a certain [man's] house, named Justus, [one] that worshipped God, <u>**whose house joined hard to the synagogue**</u>.*

NIV: Acts 18:7: Then Paul left the synagogue and went next door to the house of Titius Justus, a worshiper of God.

("<u>**whose house joined hard to the synagogue**</u>" is removed)

Acts 23:9b

*KJV...<u>**Let us not fight against God**</u>*

(NIV,modern Bible and Jehovah's Witness Bible have removed the "<u>**Let us not fight against God**</u>" Reason is obvious, there are people who dare to fight against God.)

Acts 24 :7

KJV: Acts 24:7: But the chief captain Lysias came upon us, and with great violence took him away out of our hands,

(NIV and modern version Bibles have removed this scripture completely.)

Acts 28:29

KJV: ACTS: 28:29: And when he had said these words, the Jews departed, and had great reasoning among themselves

(NIV and other versions of the Bible have removed the scripture completely. See there was a conflict there. Reasoning was about who Jesus was? So it is a must to remove this scripture.)

Elizabeth Das

Romans 1:16

*KJV: Romans1:16: For I am not ashamed of the gospel **of Christ**: for it is the power of God unto salvation to everyone that believeth; to the Jew first, and also to the Greek.*

NIV: Romans1:16: I am not ashamed of the gospel, because it is the power of God for the salvation of everyone who believes: first for the Jew, then for the Gentile.

(NIV has removed Gospel of "Christ" and kept only "Gospel". Most attacks are on Jesus as Christ. The Gospel is the death, burial and resurrection of Jesus Christ. No need for this scripture.)

Romans 8:1

*KJV: Romans 8:1: There is therefore now no condemnation to them which are in Christ Jesus, **who walk not after the flesh, but after the Spirit**.*

NIV: Romans 8:1: Therefore, there is now no condemnation for those who are in Christ Jesus

("**who walk not after the flesh, but after the Spirit**." is removed from NIV, so you can live the way you want to.)

Romans 11:6

*KJV: Roman 11:6 And if by grace, then is it no more of works: otherwise grace is no more grace. **But if it be of works, then it is no more grace: otherwise work is no more work.***

NIV: Roman 11:6 And if by grace, then it is no longer by works; if it were, grace would no longer be grace.

("But if it be of works, then it is no more grace: otherwise work is no more work." Part of the scripture is removed from NIV and other versions.)

Romans13:9b

KJV: Romans13:9b: **_Thou shalt not bear false witness_**

(NIV has removed these Words from the Scripture. The Bible says, add not, Subtract not)

Romans 16:24

KJV: Romans 16:24: The grace of our Lord Jesus Christ be with you all. Amen.

NIV: Romans 16:24: (NIV and other modern Bibles have removed the scripture completely.)

1 Corinthians 6:20

*KJV:1Corinthians 6:20: For ye are bought with a price: therefore, glorify God in your body, **and in your spirit, which are God's**.*

NIV:1Corinthians 6:20: you were bought at a price. Therefore, honor God with your bodies.

(Modern Bible and NIV has removed "and in your spirit, which are God's." our body and spirit belong to the Lord.)

1 Corinthians 7:5

*KJV:1 Corinthians 7:5: Defraud ye not one the other, except [it be] with consent for a time, that ye may give yourselves to **fasting and** *__prayer__; and come together again, that Satan tempt you not for your incontinency.*

NIV:1 Corinthians 7:5: Do not deprive each other except by mutual consent and for a time, so that you may devote yourselves to __prayer__. Then come together again so that Satan will not tempt you because of your lack of self- control.

(NIV and modern versions of the Bible have removed "fasting" since it is for pulling down the strong holds of Satan. Fasting also kills the flesh.)

2 Corinthians 6:5

KJV:2 Corinthians 6:5: In stripes, in imprisonments, in tumults, in labours, in watchings, in __fastings__;

NIV:2 Corinthians 6:5: in beatings, imprisonments and riots; in hard work, sleepless nights and __hunger__;

(**Fasting is not hunger**, changing the Word of Truth. The Devil does not want you to have a closer, powerful, deeper relation with God. Remember, Queen Esther and the Jews fasted, and God returned Satan's plan back to the enemy)

2 Corinthians 11:27

KJV: 2Corinthians 11:27: In weariness and painfulness, in watchings often, in hunger and thirst, __in fastings often__, in cold and nakedness.

NIV:2Corinthians 11:27: I have labored and toiled and have often gone without sleep; I have known hunger and thirst and have often gone without food; I have been cold and naked.

(Again, fasting is out of the NIV and modern versions of the Bible.)

Ephesians 3:9

KJV Ephesians 3:9: And to make all men see what is the fellowship of the mystery, which from the beginning of the world hath been hid in God, who created ***all things by Jesus Christ****:*

NIV Ephesians 3:9:and to make plain to everyone the administration of this mystery, which for ages past was kept hidden in God, who created all things.

(NIV and other versions of the Bible have removed "**all things by Jesus Christ**". Jesus is God and He is the Creator of all)

Ephesians 3:14

*KJV: Ephesians 3:14: For this cause I bow my knees unto the Father **of our Lord Jesus Christ**,*

NIV:Ephesians 3:14: For this reason I kneel before the Father,

("**of our Lord Jesus Christ**," is removed from NIV and other versions. This is the proof that Jesus is the Son of God. The "Son of God" is a Mighty God in flesh who came to shed the blood for you and me. Remember Satan believes there is one God and trembles. James 2:19)

Ephesians 5:30

*KJV:Ephesians 5:30:For we are members of his body, of his flesh, and **of his bones**.*

NIV:Ephesians 5:30:for we are members of his body.

("**Of flesh, and of his bones**." Part of the Scripture is removed from the NIV and many other versions of the Bible.)

Colossians 1:14

*KJV:Colossians 1:14: In whom we have redemption **through his blood**, even the forgiveness of sins:*

NIV:Colossians 1:14: in whom we have redemption, the forgiveness of sins.

("**through his blood**," Jesus is called The Lamb of God who came to take away the sins of this world. Redemption is **only** through the blood. Without shedding blood there is no remission of sins Hebrew 9:22. That is why we baptize in the name of Jesus, to apply His blood over our sins.)

1 Timothy 3:16b

*KJV:1 Timothy 3:16b: **God was** manifest in the flesh*

*NIV:1 Timothy 3:16b: **He** appeared in a body.*

(Don't we all appear in a body? NIV and most modern versions all says "he" appeared in a body. Well, I appear in a body too. "He" who? In the above verse they are again changing the wording to amply "He" is another god. But in KJV, we can clearly see "And without controversy great is the mystery of godliness: "**God** was manifest in the flesh." There is only one God. That is why Jesus said if you have seen me you have seen the Father. The Father is a spirit, you cannot see spirit. But the spirit robed itself in flesh you could see it.)

*Acts 20:28b Says: To feed the **church of God**, which he hath purchased with his **own blood**.*

God is a spirit, and to shed blood, he needs a flesh and blood body. **One God** who put on the flesh.

Simple example: Ice, water, and steam, same thing but a different manifestation.

*KJV 1 John 5: 7: "For there are three that bear record in heaven, the Father, the Word, and the Holy Ghost: and these **three are one**."*

God, Jesus (Word become flesh) and Holy Spirit are one not three. (1 John 5:7 is completly removed from NIV and other current translations.)

2 Timothy 3:16

*KJV: 2 Timothy 3:16: **All** scripture is given by inspiration of God, and is profitable for doctrine, for reproof, for correction, for instruction in righteousness:*

*ASV: 2 Timothy 3:16: **Every** scripture inspired of God is also profitable for teaching.*

(Here they will decide which one is and which one is not. Heresy will be put to death.)

1 Thessalonians 1:1

*KJV: 1 Thessalonians 1:1: Paul, and Silvanus, and Timotheus, unto the church of the Thessalonians which is in God the Father and in the Lord Jesus Christ: Grace be unto you, and peace, **from God our Father, and the Lord Jesus Christ**.*

NIV:1 Thessalonians 1:1: Paul, Silas and Timothy, To the church of the Thessalonians in God the Father and the Lord Jesus Christ: Grace and peace to you.

("from God our Father, and the Lord Jesus Christ." is removed from modern translations and NIV.)

Hebrews 7:21

*KJV: Hebrews 7:21: (**For those priests were made without an oath**; but this with an oath by him that said unto him, The Lord sware and* *will not repent, Thou art a priest for ever **after the order of Melchisedec**):*

*NIV: Hebrews 7:21: but he became a priest **with an oath** when God said to him:"The Lord has sworn and will not change his mind: ' You are a priest forever.'"*

(NIV has removed the "For those priests were made without an oath" and "after the order of Melchisedec".)

James 5:16

*KJV: James 5:16: Confess your **faults** one to another, and pray one for another, that ye may be healed. The effectual fervent prayer of a righteous man availeth much.*

*NIV: James 5:16: Therefore, confess your **sins** to each other and pray for each other so that you may be healed. The prayer of a righteous man is powerful and effective.*

(**Faults vs. Sins**: Sins you confess to God since He alone can forgive. Changing the word "faults to sins" helps support the Catholic view of confessing "sins" to a priest.)

1 Peter 1:22

*KJV: 1 Peter 1:22: seeing ye have purified your souls in obeying the truth **through the Spirit unto** unfeigned love of the brethren, see that ye love one another with a **pure heart fervently**:*

NIV: 1 Peter 1:22: Now that you have purified yourselves by obeying the truth so that you have sincere love for your brothers, love one another deeply, from the heart.

("**through the Spirit unto**" and "**pure heart fervently**" is removed from NIV and other modern versions.)

1 Peter 4:14

KJV:1 Peter 4:14: If ye be reproached for the name of Christ, happy are ye; for the spirit of glory and of God resteth upon you: **on their part he is evil spoken of, but on your part he is glorified.**

NIV:1 Peter 4:14: If you are insulted because of the name of Christ, you are blessed, for the spirit of glory and of God rests on you.

("**on their part he is evil spoken of, but on your part he is glorified**." is removed from NIV and other modern versions.)

1 John 4:3a

KJV:1 John 4:3a: And every spirit that confesseth not that Jesus **Christ is come in the flesh** *is not of God.*

NIV:1 John 4:3a: But every spirit that does not acknowledge Jesus is not from God.

("**Christ is come in the flesh**" By removing these words, NIV and other versions proves that they are antichrist.)

1 John 5:7-8

KJV: 1 John 5:7: **For there are three that bear record in heaven, the Father, the Word, and the Holy Ghost: and these three are one.**

(Removed from NIV)

KJV: 1 John 5:8: And there are three that bear witness in earth, the Spirit, and the water, and the blood: and these three agree in one.

NIV: 1 John 5:7, 8: **For there are three that testify:** *8 the Spirit, the water and the blood; and the three are in agreement*

(This is one of the GREATEST verses testifying of the Godhead. One God, not three gods. The **Trinity** is not Biblical. The word **Trinity** is not in the Bible. That is why NIV, modern versions of the Bible and the Jehovah's Witnesses has omitted it out of this verse. They do not believe in the Godhead and they do not believe that in Jesus, dwells all the fullness of the Godhead bodily. There is no root or evidence in the Bible whatsoever for the acceptance of the **Trinity**. Why does the NIV leave it out...? Whole books have been written on the manuscript evidence that supports inclusion of this verse in the Bible. Do you believe in the Godhead? If so, then this removal should offend you. The Trinity was never taught by Jesus and was never mentioned by Him. Satan divided one God so he can divide people and rule.)

1 John 5:13

*KJV:1John 5:13: These things have I written unto you that believe on the name of the Son of God; that ye may know that ye have eternal life, **and that ye may believe on the name of the Son of God**.*

NIV:1John 5:13: I write these things to you who believe in the name of the Son of God so that you may know that you have eternal life.

("**and that ye may believe on the name of the Son of God**." Is removed from NIV and other modern translations)

Revelation 1:8

*KJV: Revelation1:8: I am Alpha and Omega, **the beginning and the ending**, saith the Lord, which is, and which was, and which is to come, the Almighty*

NIV: Revelation1:8: "I am the Alpha and the Omega," says the Lord God, "who is, and who was, and who is to come, the Almighty."

(NIV removed **the beginning and the ending**)

Revelation 1:11

KJV:Revelation 1:11:<u>Saying, I am Alpha and Omega, the first and the last: and, What thou seest, write in a book, and send it unto the seven churches which are in Asia</u>; unto Ephesus, and unto Smyrna, and unto Pergamos, and unto Thyatira, and unto Sardis, and unto Philadelphia, and unto Laodicea

NIV: Revelation 1:11: which said: "Write on a scroll what you see and send it to the seven churches: to Ephesus, Smyrna, Pergamum, Thyatira, Sardis, Philadelphia and Laodicea."

(Alpha and Omega, beginning and the ending and first and last; these titles are given to Jehovah God in the Old Testament and in Revelation it is also given to Jesus. But the NIV and other modern versions, have removed this from Revelation to prove that Jesus is not the Jehovah God.)

Revelation 5:14

KJV:Revelation 5:14: And the <u>four beasts</u> said, Amen. And the <u>four and twenty</u> elders fell down and worshipped him <u>that liveth for ever and ever</u>.

NIV: Revelation 5:14: The four living creatures said, "Amen," and the elders fell down and worshiped.

(NIV and other versions provide only half of the information. "**four beasts**", changed to four creatures," **four and twenty**", "that liveth for ever and ever" is removed.)

Revelation 20:9b

KJV: Revelation 20:9b: Fire came down <u>from God</u> out of heaven.

NIV: Revelation 20:9b: Fire came down from heaven

Elizabeth Das

(NIV and other versions have removed "**from God**".)

Revelation 21:24a

*KJV: Revelation 21:24a: And the nations **of them which are saved** shall walk in the light of it.*

NIV: Revelation 21:24a: The nations will walk by its light.

("**of them which are saved**" is removed from NIV and modern versions of the Bible. Everyone is not going to heaven but those who are saved.)

2 Samuel 21:19

*KJV: 2 Samuel 21:19: And there was again a battle in Gob with the Philistines, where Elhanan the son of Jaareoregim, a Bethlehemite, slew the **brother of Goliath** the Gittite, the staff of whose spear was like a weaver's beam.*

*NIV:2 Samuel 21:19: In another battle with the Philistines at Gob, Elhanan son of Jaare-Oregim the Bethlehemite **killed Goliath** the Gittite, who had a spear with a shaft like a weaver's rod.*

(Goliath's brother was killed here not Goliath. "David killed Goliath." NIV misrepresents the information.)

Hosea 11:12

*KJV: Hosea 11:12: Ephraim compasseth me about with lies, and the house of Israel with deceit: **but Judah yet ruleth with God, and is faithful** with the saints.*

*NIV: Hosea 11:12: Ephraim has surrounded me with lies, the house of Israel with deceit. And Judah is **unruly against** God, even **against** the faithful Holy One.*

(The NIV misrepresents this scripture by twisting the meaning of the word.) The Word "Jehovah" is mentioned four times in the KJV Bible. The NIV removed all of them. With subtle CHANGES being made in the NIV Bible, Satan's mission becomes clear. From the above scriptures you can see, that the attack is on Jesus. The titles God, Messiah, Son of God, and Creator make Jesus, God. By removing these titles, confusion makes you lose interest and not trust the Word of God. (I Corinthians 14:33 For God is not the author of confusion, but of peace.)

The Jehovah's Witness Bible, (the New World Translation) has the same deletions that the NIV has. The only difference between the NIV and the New World Translation deletions is that the Jehovah's Witness Bible does not include any footnotes! These methods are desensitizing you to the subtle changes that are gradually and continually being made to God's Word.

Today's busy and lazy generation has influenced many professing Christians who have embraced the ways of a slothful spirit. It is hard work, to take the time to study and make sure that information given to us, is true. We have become too busy with everyday life which is full of unimportant events and things. Our priorities for what is really important for eternal life have been diluted and confused. We are accepting most of the information given to us, without question; whether it is from government, medical, scientific, contents of our food, and the list goes on.

Many of our modern Bible versions have been written by men that are telling you their interpretation and their doctrine instead of what the manuscripts really say. For example, "gender inclusivity" was not in the original manuscripts. It is a modern feminist concept born of REBELLION. I encourage you to get a King James Version Bible. If you read a modern Bible, take the time to compare scriptures; desire to make the right decision. We will be held accountable for our decisions. The difference of going to Heaven or Hell is reason enough to make sure you are choosing His Word! Remember, that the New International Version deletes many words such as: Godhead, regeneration, remission, immutable, Jehovah, Calvary, mercy seat, Holy Ghost, Comforter, Messiah, quickened, omnipotent, infallible, et cetera. Most of the modern Bibles line up closely with the NIV; along with the New World Translation Bible (the Bible of the Jehovah's Witnesses').

This is the work of the Antichrist....(Following Scriptures are taken from KJV)

*Little children, it is the last time: and as ye have heard that **antichrist** shall come, even now are there many **antichrists**; whereby we know that it is the last time. (1 John 2:18)*

*Who is a liar but he that denieth that Jesus is the Christ? He is **antichrist**, that denieth the Father and the Son. (1 John 2:22)*

*And every spirit that confesseth not that Jesus Christ is come in the flesh is not of God: and this is that spirit of **antichrist**, whereof ye have heard that it should come; and even now already is it in the world. (1 John 4:3)*

*For many deceivers are entered into the world, who confess not that Jesus Christ is come in the flesh. This is a deceiver and an **antichrist**. (2 John 1:7)*

This reminds us of the "PARABLE OF THE SEED" WHICH IS THE "WORD OF GOD" in the Bible

Another parable put the forth unto them, saying, The kingdom of heaven is likened unto a man which sowed good seed in his field: But while men slept, his enemy came and sowed tares among the wheat, and went his way. But when the blade was sprung up, and brought forth fruit, then appeared the tares also. So the servants of the householder came and said unto him, Sir, didst not thou sow good seed in thy field? from whence then hath it tears? He said unto them, an enemy hath done this. The servants said unto him, wilt thou then that

we go and gather them up? But he said, Nay; lest while ye gather up the tares, ye root up also the wheat with them. Let both grow together until the harvest: and in the time of harvest I will say to the reapers, gather ye together first the tares, and bind them in bundles to burn them: but gather the wheat into my barn. Amen!
(Mathew 13:24-30)

AMEN!

www.ingramcontent.com/pod-product-compliance
Lightning Source LLC
Chambersburg PA
CBHW071414090426
42737CB00011B/1457